New Perspectives on
Microsoft®
Excel 97

BRIEF

June Jamrich Parsons
University of the Virgin Islands

Dan Oja
GuildWare, Inc.

Roy Ageloff
University of Rhode Island

COURSE
TECHNOLOGY

ONE MAIN STREET, CAMBRIDGE, MA 02142

an International Thomson Publishing company I(T)P®

Cambridge • Albany • Bonn • Boston • Cincinnati • London • Madrid • Melbourne • Mexico City
New York • Paris • San Francisco • Singapore • Tokyo • Toronto • Washington

New Perspectives on Microsoft® Excel 97 — Brief is published by Course Technology.

Associate Publisher	Mac Mendelsohn
Series Consulting Editor	Susan Solomon
Product Manager	Mark Reimold
Developmental Editor	Kim T.M. Crowley
Production Editor	Nancy Ray
Text and Cover Designer	Ella Hanna
Cover Illustrator	Douglas Goodman

© 1997 by Course Technology
A Division of International Thomson Publishing — I(T)P®

For more information contact:

Course Technology
One Main Street
Cambridge, MA 02142

International Thomson Publishing Europe
Berkshire House 168-173
High Holborn
London WCIV 7AA
England

Thomas Nelson Australia
102 Dodds Street
South Melbourne, 3205
Victoria, Australia

Nelson Canada
1120 Birchmount Road
Scarborough, Ontario
Canada M1K 5G4

International Thomson Editores
Campos Eliseos 385, Piso 7
Col. Polanco
11560 Mexico D.F. Mexico

International Thomson Publishing GmbH
Königswinterer Strasse 418
53227 Bonn
Germany

International Thomson Publishing Asia
211 Henderson Road
#05-10 Henderson Building
Singapore 0315

International Thomson Publishing Japan
Hirakawacho Kyowa Building, 3F
2-2-1 Hirakawacho
Chiyoda-ku, Tokyo 102
Japan

ISBN 0-7600-4553-4

Printed in the United States of America

10 9 8 7 6 5 4

Preface The New Perspectives Series

What is the New Perspectives Series?

Course Technology's **New Perspectives Series** is an integrated system of instruction that combines text and technology products to teach computer concepts and micro-computer applications. Users consistently praise this series for innovative pedagogy, creativity, supportive and engaging style, accuracy, and use of interactive technology. The first New Perspectives text was published in January of 1993. Since then, the series has grown to more than 100 titles and has become the best-selling series on computer concepts and microcomputer applications. Others have imitated the New Perspectives features, design, and technologies, but none have replicated its quality and its ability to consistently anticipate and meet the needs of instructors and students.

How does this book I'm holding fit into the New Perspectives Series?

New Perspectives applications books are available in the following categories:

Brief books are typically about 160 pages long, contain two to four tutorials, and are intended to teach the basics of an application. The book you are holding is a Brief book.

Introductory books are typically about 300 pages long and consist of four to seven tutorials that go beyond the basics. These books often build out of the Brief editions by providing two or three additional tutorials.

Comprehensive books are typically about 600 pages long and consist of all of the tutorials in the Introductory books, plus four or five more tutorials covering high-er-level topics. Comprehensive books also include two Windows tutorials, three or four Additional Cases, and a References section.

Advanced books cover topics similar to those in the Comprehensive books, but go into more depth. Advanced books present the most high-level coverage in the series.

Custom Books offer you two ways to customize a New Perspectives text to fit your course exactly: *CourseKits*™, two or more texts packaged together in a box, and *Custom Editions*®, your choice of books bound together. Custom Editions offer you unparalleled flexibility in designing your concepts and applications courses. You can build your own book by ordering a combination of titles bound together to cover only the topics you want. Your students save because they buy only the materials they need. There is no minimum order, and books are spiral bound. Both CourseKits and Custom Editions offer significant price discounts. Contact your Course Technology sales representative for more information.

New Perspectives Series Microcomputer Applications

■ Brief Titles or Modules	■ Introductory Titles or Modules	■ Intermediate Tutorials	■ Advanced Titles or Modules	□ Other Modules

Brief	Introductory	Comprehensive	Advanced	Custom Editions
2 to 4 tutorials	6 or 7 tutorials, or Brief + 2 or 3 more tutorials	Introductory + 4 or 5 more tutorials. Includes Brief Windows tutorials, Additional Cases, and References section	Quick Review of basics + in-depth, high-level coverage	Choose from any of the above to build your own Custom Editions® or CourseKits™

How do the Windows 95 editions differ from the Windows 3.1 editions?

Sessions We've divided the tutorials into sessions. Each session is designed to be completed in about 45 minutes to an hour (depending, of course, upon student needs and the speed of your lab equipment). With sessions, learning is broken up into more easily-assimilated portions. You can more accurately allocate time in your syllabus, and students can better manage the available lab time. Each session begins with a "session box," which quickly describes the skills students will learn in the session. Furthermore, each session is numbered, which makes it easier for you and your students to navigate and communicate about the tutorial. Look on page E 2.18 for the session box that opens Session 2.2.

Quick Checks Each session concludes with meaningful, conceptual Quick Check questions that test students' understanding of what they learned in the session. Answers to all of the Quick Check questions in this book are provided on pages E 4.38 through E 4.40.

New Design We have retained the best of the old design to help students differentiate between what they are to *do* and what they are to *read*. The steps are clearly identified by their shaded background and numbered steps. Furthermore, this new design presents steps and screen shots in a larger, easier to read format. Some good examples of our new design are pages E 1.12 and E 1.13.

What features are retained in the Windows 95 editions of the New Perspectives Series?

"Read This Before You Begin" Page This page is consistent with Course Technology's unequaled commitment to helping instructors introduce technology into the classroom. Technical considerations and assumptions about software are listed to help instructors save time and eliminate unnecessary aggravation. See page E 1.2 for the "Read This Before You Begin" page in this book.

Tutorial Case Each tutorial begins with a problem presented in a case that is meaningful to students. The problem turns the task of learning how to use an application into a problem-solving process. The problems increase in complexity with each tutorial. These cases touch on multicultural, international, and ethical issues—so important to today's business curriculum. See page E 1.3 for the case that begins Tutorial 1.

Step-by-Step Methodology This unique Course Technology methodology keeps students on track. They enter data, click buttons, or press keys always within the context of solving the problem posed in the tutorial case. The text constantly guides students, letting them know where they are in the course of solving the problem. In addition, the numerous screen shots include labels that direct students' attention to what they should look at on the screen. On almost every page in this book, you can find an example of how steps, screen shots, and labels work together.

TROUBLE?

TROUBLE? Paragraphs These paragraphs anticipate the mistakes or problems that students are likely to have and help them recover and continue with the tutorial. By putting these paragraphs in the book, rather than in the Instructor's Manual, we facilitate independent learning and free the instructor to focus on substantive conceptual issues rather than on common procedural errors. Two representative examples of Trouble? paragraphs are on pages E 1.6 and E 1.11.

Reference Windows Reference Windows appear throughout the text. They are succinct summaries of the most important tasks covered in the tutorials. Reference Windows are specially designed and written so students can refer to them when doing the Tutorial Assignments and Case Problems, and after completing the course. Page E 2.19 contains the Reference Window for Using the Paste Function Button.

Task Reference The Task Reference contains a summary of how to perform common tasks using the most efficient method, as well as references to pages where the task is discussed in more detail. It appears as a table at the end of the book.

Tutorial Assignments, Case Problems, and Lab Assignments Each tutorial concludes with Tutorial Assignments, which provide students with additional hands-on practice of the skills they learned in the tutorial. See pages E 1.32 and E 1.33 for examples of Tutorial Assignments. The Tutorial Assignments are followed by four Case Problems that have approximately the same scope as the tutorial case. In the Windows 95 applications texts, the last Case Problem of each tutorial typically requires students to solve the problem independently, either "from scratch" or with minimum guidance. See pages E 1.33 through E 1.35 for examples of Case Problems. Finally, if a Course Lab accompanies a tutorial, Lab Assignments are included after the Case Problems. See page E 1.35 for the Spreadsheets Lab Assignments.

Exploration Exercises The Windows environment allows students to learn by exploring and discovering what they can do. Exploration Exercises can be Tutorial Assignments or Case Problems that challenge students, encourage them to explore the capabilities of the program they are using, and extend their knowledge using the Help facility and other reference materials. Page E 1.33 contains Exploration Exercises for Tutorial 1.

What supplements are available with this textbook?

Course Labs: Now, Concepts Come to Life Computer skills and concepts come to life with the New Perspectives Course Labs—highly-interactive tutorials that combine illustrations, animations, digital images, and simulations. The Labs guide students step-by-step, present them with Quick Check questions, let them explore on their own, test their comprehension, and provide printed feedback. Lab icons at the beginning of the tutorial and in the tutorial margins indicate when a topic has a corresponding Lab. Lab Assignments are included at the end of each relevant tutorial. The Lab available with this book and the tutorial in which it appears is:

Tutorial 1

Course Test Manager: Testing and Practice at the Computer or on Paper Course Test Manager is cutting-edge Windows-based testing software that helps instructors design and administer practice tests and actual examinations. This full-featured program allows students to randomly generate practice tests that provide immediate on-screen feedback and detailed study guides. Instructors can also use Course Test Manager to produce printed tests. Course Test Manager can automatically grade the tests students take at the computer and can generate statistical information on individual as well as group performance.

Online Companions: Dedicated to Keeping You and Your Students Up-To-Date
When you use a New Perspectives product, you can access Course Technology's faculty sites and student sites on the World Wide Web. You can browse the password-protected Faculty Online Companions to obtain online Instructor's Manuals, Solution Files, Student Files, and more. Please see your Instructor's Manual or call your Course Technology customer service representative for more information. Student and Faculty Online Companions are accessible by clicking the appropriate links on Course Technology's home page at **http://www.course.com.**

Instructor's Manual New Perspectives Series Instructor's Manuals contain instructor's notes and printed solutions for each tutorial. Instructor's notes provide tutorial overviews and outlines, technical notes, lecture notes, and extra case problems. Printed solutions include solutions to Tutorial Assignments, Case Problems, and Lab Assignments.

Internet Assignments The Instructor's Manual that accompanies this text includes additional assignments that integrate the World Wide Web with the spreadsheet skills students learn in the tutorials. To complete these assignments, students will need to search the Web and follow the links from the New Perspectives on Microsoft Office 97 home page. The Office 97 home page is accessible through the Student Online Companions link found on the Course Technology home page at **http:\\www.course.com.** Please refer to the Instructor's Manual for more information.

Student Files Student Files contain all of the data that students will use to complete the tutorials, Tutorial Assignments, and Case Problems. A Readme file includes technical tips for lab management. See the inside covers of this book and the "Read This Before You Begin" page before Tutorial 1 for more information on Student Files.

Solution Files Solution Files contain every file students are asked to create or modify in the tutorials, Tutorial Assignments, and Case Problems.

The following supplements are included in the Instructor's Resource Kit that accompanies this textbook:

- Instructor's Manual
- Solution Files
- Student Files
- Spreadsheets Course Lab
- Course Test Manager Release 1.1 Test Bank
- Course Test Manager Release 1.1 Engine

Some of the supplements listed above are also available over the World Wide Web through Course Technology's password-protected Faculty Online Companions. Please see your Instructor's Manual or call your Course Technology customer service representative for more information.

Acknowledgments

Many thanks to the New Perspectives team at Course Technology, particularly Mac Mendelsohn, Associate Publisher; Susan Solomon, Series Consulting Editor; Mark Reimold, Product Manager; Nancy Ray, Production Editor; Greg Bigelow, Quality Assurance Project Leader; John McCarthy, QA Manuscript Reviewer; Brian McCooey, QA Manuscript Reviewer; Patty Stephan, Production Manager; and Kim Crowley, Development Editor.

Also, thank you to Calleen Coorough, Skafit Valley College, Nancy Alderice, Murray State University, and Jean Smelewicz, Quinsigamond Community College, for their insightful reviews of the manuscript.

June Jamrich Parsons
Dan Oja
Roy Ageloff

Table of **Contents**

Microsoft® Excel 97

LEVEL I

TUTORIALS

Read This **Before You Begin**

Using Worksheets to Make Business Decisions

Evaluating Sites for an Inwood Design Group Golf Course

Excel

OBJECTIVES

In this tutorial you will:

- Start and exit Excel

- Discover how Excel is used in business

- Identify the major components of the Excel window

- Navigate an Excel workbook and worksheet

- Open, save, print, and close a worksheet

- Enter text, numbers, formulas, and functions

- Correct mistakes

- Perform what-if analysis

- Clear contents of cells

- Use the Excel Help system

LAB
Spreadsheets

CASE

Inwood Design Group

In Japan, golf is big business. Spurred by the Japanese passion for the sport, golf enjoys unprecedented popularity. But because Japan is a small, mountainous country, the 12 million golfers have fewer than 2,000 courses from which to choose. Fees for 18 holes on a public course average between $200 and $300; golf club memberships are bought and sold like stock shares. The market potential is phenomenal, but building a golf course in Japan is expensive because of inflated property values, difficult terrain, and strict environmental regulations.

Inwood Design Group plans to build a world-class golf course, and one of the four sites under consideration is Chiba Prefecture, Japan. Other possible sites are Kauai, Hawaii; Edmonton, Canada; and Scottsdale, Arizona. You and Mike Nagochi are members of the site selection team for Inwood Design Group. The team is responsible for collecting information on the sites, evaluating that information, and recommending the best site for the new golf course.

Your team identified five factors likely to determine the success of a golf course: climate, competition, market size, topography, and transportation. The team has already collected information on these factors for three of the four potential golf course sites. Mike has just returned from visiting the last site in Scottsdale, Arizona.

Using Microsoft Excel 97 for Windows 95, Mike has created a worksheet that the team can use to evaluate the four sites. He needs to complete the worksheet by entering the data for the Scottsdale site. He then plans to bring the worksheet to the group's next meeting so that the team can analyze the information and recommend a site to management.

In this tutorial you will learn how to use Excel as you work with Mike to complete the Inwood site selection worksheet and work with the Inwood team to select the best site for the golf course.

Using the Tutorials Effectively

These tutorials are designed to be used at a computer. Each tutorial is divided into sessions. Watch for the session headings, such as "Session 1.1" and "Session 1.2." Each session is designed to be completed in about 45 minutes, but take as much time as you need. When you've completed a session, it's a good idea to exit the program and take a break. You can exit Microsoft Excel by clicking the Close button in the top-right corner of the program window.

Before you begin, read the following questions and answers. They are designed to help you use the tutorials effectively.

Where do I start?

Each tutorial begins with a case, which sets the scene for the tutorial and gives you background information to help you understand what you will be doing in the tutorial. Read the case before you go to the lab. In the lab, begin with the first session of the tutorial.

How do I know what to do on the computer?

Each session contains steps that you will perform on the computer to learn how to use Microsoft Excel. The steps are numbered and are set against a colored background. Read the text that introduces each series of steps, and read each step carefully and completely before you try it.

How do I know if I did the step correctly?

As you work, compare your computer screen with the corresponding figure in the tutorial. Don't worry if your screen display is somewhat different from the figure. The important parts of the screen display are labeled in each figure. Check to make sure these parts are on your screen.

What if I make a mistake?

Don't worry about making mistakes—they are part of the learning process. Paragraphs labeled **TROUBLE?** identify common problems and explain how to get back on track. Follow the steps in a **TROUBLE?** paragraph *only* if you are having the problem described. If you run into other problems, carefully consider the current state of your system, the position of the pointer, and any messages on the screen.

How do I use the Reference Windows?

Reference Windows summarize the procedures you learn in the tutorial steps. Do not complete the actions in the Reference Windows when you are working through the tutorial. Instead, refer to the Reference Windows while you are working on the assignments at the end of the tutorial.

How can I test my understanding of the material I learned in the tutorial?

At the end of each session, you can answer the Quick Check Questions. If necessary, refer to the Answers to Quick Check Questions to check your work.

After you have completed the entire tutorial, you should complete the Tutorial Assignments and Case Problems. These exercises are carefully structured so you will review what you have learned and then apply your knowledge to new situations.

What if I can't remember how to do something?

You should refer to the Task Reference at the end of the book; it summarizes how to accomplish commonly performed tasks.

What is the Spreadsheets Course Lab, and how should I use it?

This interactive Lab helps you review spreadsheet concepts and practice skills that you learn in Tutorial 1. The Lab Assignments section at the end of Tutorial 1 includes instructions for using the Lab.

Now that you've seen how to use the tutorials effectively, you are ready to begin.

SESSION

1.1

In this session you will learn what a spreadsheet is and how it is used in business. You will learn what Excel is and about the Excel window and its elements, how to move around a worksheet using the keyboard and the mouse, and how to open a workbook.

Spreadsheets

What Is Excel?

Excel is a computerized spreadsheet. A **spreadsheet** is an important business tool that helps you analyze and evaluate information. Spreadsheets are often used for cash flow analysis, budgeting, decision making, cost estimating, inventory management, and financial reporting. For example, an accountant might use a spreadsheet like the one in Figure 1-1 for a budget.

Figure 1-1
Budget
spreadsheet

Cash Budget Forecast		
	January Estimated	January Actual
Cash in Bank (Start of Month)	$1,400.00	$1,400.00
Cash in Register (Start of Month)	100.00	100.00
Total Cash	$1,500.00	$1,500.00
Expected Cash Sales	$1,200.00	$1,420.00
Expected Collections	400.00	380.00
Other Money Expected	100.00	52.00
Total Income	$1,700.00	$1,852.00
Total Cash and Income	$3,200.00	$3,352.00
All Expenses (for Month)	$1,200.00	$1,192.00
Cash Balance at End of Month	$2,000.00	$2,160.00

To produce the spreadsheet in Figure 1-1, you could manually calculate the totals and then type your results, or you could use a computer and spreadsheet program to perform the calculations and print the results. Spreadsheet programs are also referred to as electronic spreadsheets, computerized spreadsheets, or just spreadsheets.

In Excel 97, the document you create is called a **workbook**. Each workbook is made up of individual worksheets, or **sheets**, just as a spiral-bound notebook is made up of sheets of paper. You will learn more about using multiple sheets later in this tutorial. For now, just keep in mind that the terms *worksheet* and *sheet* are often used interchangeably.

Starting Excel

Mike arrives at his office early because he needs to work with you to finish the worksheet and get ready for your meeting with the design team.

Start Excel and complete the worksheet that Mike will use to help the design team decide about the golf course site.

To start Microsoft Excel:

1. Make sure Windows 95 is running on your computer and the Windows 95 desktop appears on your screen.

TROUBLE? If you're running Windows NT Workstation 4.0 (or a later version) on your computer or network, don't worry. Although the figures in this book were created while running Windows 95, Windows NT 4.0 and Windows 95 share the same interface, and Microsoft Excel 97 runs equally well under either systems.

2. Click the **Start** button on the taskbar to display the Start menu, and then point to **Programs** to display the Programs menu.

3. Point to **Microsoft Excel** on the Programs menu. See Figure 1-2.

Figure 1-2 ◀
Starting
Microsoft Excel

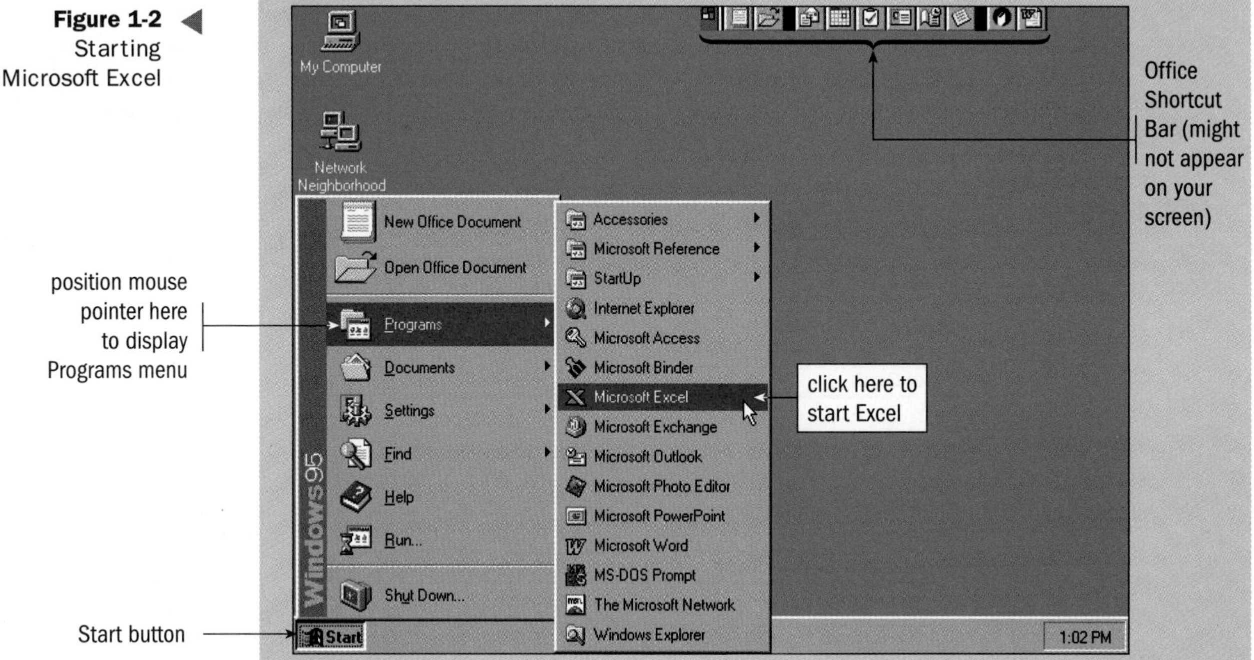

position mouse
pointer here
to display
Programs menu

Start button

Office
Shortcut
Bar (might
not appear
on your
screen)

click here to
start Excel

TROUBLE? If you don't see the Microsoft Excel option on the Programs menu, ask your instructor or technical support person for assistance.

TROUBLE? The Office Shortcut Bar, which appears along the top border of the desktop in Figure 1-2, might look different on your screen or it might not appear at all, depending on how your system is set up. The steps in these tutorials do not require that you use the Office Shortcut Bar; therefore, the remaining figures do not display the Office Shortcut Bar.

4. Click **Microsoft Excel**. After a short pause, the Microsoft Excel copyright information appears in a message box and remains on the screen until the Excel program window and a blank worksheet are displayed. See Figure 1-3.

TROUBLE? Depending on how your system is set up, the Office Assistant (see Figure 1-3) window might open when you start Excel. For now, click the Close button ⊠ on the Office Assistant window to close it; you'll learn more about this feature later in this tutorial. If you've started Microsoft Excel immediately after installing it, you'll need to click the Start Using Microsoft Excel option, which the Office Assistant displays, before closing the Office Assistant window.

Excel

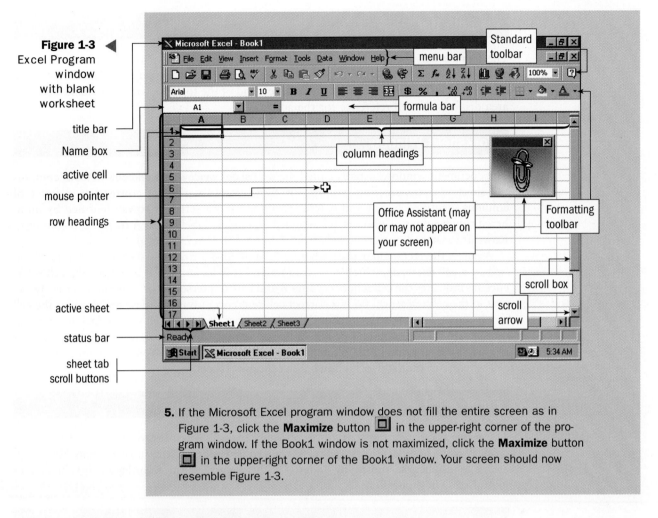

Figure 1-3
Excel Program
window
with blank
worksheet

title bar

Name box

active cell

mouse pointer

row headings

active sheet

status bar

sheet tab
scroll buttons

Standard toolbar

menu bar

formula bar

column headings

Office Assistant (may or may not appear on your screen)

Formatting toolbar

scroll box

scroll arrow

5. If the Microsoft Excel program window does not fill the entire screen as in Figure 1-3, click the **Maximize** button [ ] in the upper-right corner of the program window. If the Book1 window is not maximized, click the **Maximize** button [ ] in the upper-right corner of the Book1 window. Your screen should now resemble Figure 1-3.

The Excel Window

The Excel window layout is consistent with the layout of other Windows programs. It contains many common features, such as the title bar, menu bar, scroll bars, and taskbar. Figure 1-3 shows these elements as well as the main components of the Excel window. Take a look at each of these Excel components so you know their location and purpose.

Toolbars

Toolbars allow you to organize the commands in Excel. The menu bar is a special toolbar at the top of the window that contains menus such as File, Edit, and View. The Standard toolbar and the Formatting toolbar are located below the menu bar. The **Standard** toolbar contains buttons corresponding to the most frequently used commands in Excel. The **Formatting** toolbar contains buttons corresponding to the commands most frequently used to improve the appearance of a worksheet.

Formula Bar

The **formula bar**, located immediately below the toolbars, displays the contents of the active cell. A **cell's contents** is the data you enter into it. As you type or edit data, the changes appear in the formula bar. At the left end of the formula bar is the **Name box.** This area displays the cell reference for the active cell.

Worksheet Window

The document window, usually called the **worksheet window** or **workbook window**, contains the sheet you are creating, editing, or using. Each worksheet consists of a series of columns identified by lettered column headings and a series of rows identified by numbered row headings. Columns are assigned alphabetic labels from A to IV (256 columns). Rows are assigned numeric labels from 1 to 65,536 (65,536 rows).

A **cell** is the rectangular area where a column and a row intersect. Each cell is identified by a **cell reference**, which is its column and row location. For example, the cell reference B6 indicates the cell where column B and row 6 intersect. The column letter is always first in the cell reference. B6 is a correct cell reference; 6B is not. The **active cell** is the cell in which you are currently working. Excel identifies the active cell with a dark border that outlines one cell. In Figure 1-3, cell A1 is the active cell. Notice that the cell reference for the active cell appears in the reference area of the formula bar. You can change the active cell when you want to work elsewhere in the worksheet.

Pointer

The **pointer** is the indicator that moves on your screen as you move your mouse. The pointer changes shape to reflect the type of task you can perform at a particular location. When you click a mouse button, something happens at the pointer's location. In Figure 1-3 the pointer looks like a white plus sign ✛ .

Sheet Tabs

The **sheet tabs** let you move quickly between the sheets in a workbook; you can simply check the sheet tab of the sheet you want to move to. By default, a new workbook consists of three worksheets. If your workbook contains many worksheets, you can use the **sheet tab scroll buttons** to scroll through the sheet tabs that are not currently visible to find the sheet you want.

Moving Around a Worksheet

Before entering or editing the contents of a cell, you need to select that cell to make it the active cell. You can select a cell using either the keyboard or the mouse.

Using the Mouse

Using the mouse, you can quickly select a cell by placing the mouse pointer on the cell and clicking the mouse button. If you need to move to a cell that's not currently on the screen, use the vertical and horizontal scroll bars to display the area of the worksheet containing the cell you are interested in, and then select the cell.

Using the Keyboard

In addition to the mouse, Excel provides you with many keyboard options for moving to different cell locations within your worksheet. Figure 1-4 shows some of the keys you can use to select a cell within your worksheet.

Excel

Figure 1-4 ◄
Keys to move
around the
worksheet

Keystroke	Action
↑, ↓, ←, →	Moves up, down, left, or right one cell
PgUp	Moves the active cell up one full screen
PgDn	Moves the active cell down one full screen
Home	Moves the active cell to column A of the current row
Ctrl + Home	Moves the active cell to cell A1

Now, try moving around the worksheet using your keyboard and mouse.

To move around the worksheet:

1. Position the mouse pointer ▷ over cell E8, then click the **left mouse** button to make it the active cell. Notice that the cell is surrounded by a black border to indicate that it is the active cell and that the Name box on the formula bar displays E8.

2. Click cell **B4** to make it the active cell.

3. Press the → key to make cell C4 the active cell.

4. Press the ↓ key to make cell C5 the active cell. See Figure 1-5.

Figure 1-5 ◄
Cell C5 as
active cell

active cell ──────→

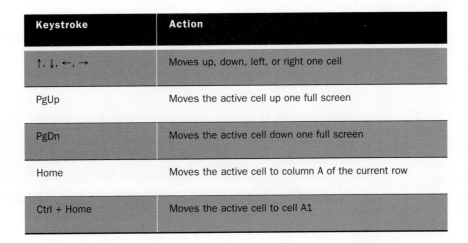

5. Press the **Home** key to move to cell A5, the first cell in the current row.

6. Press **Ctrl + Home** to make cell A1 the active cell.

So far you've moved around the portion of the worksheet you can see. Many worksheets can't be viewed entirely on one screen. Next, you'll use the keyboard and mouse to move beyond the worksheet window.

To move beyond the worksheet window:

1. Press the **Page Down** key to move the display down one screen. The active cell is now cell A17 (the active cell on your screen may be different). Notice that the row numbers on the left side of the worksheet indicate you have moved to a different area of the worksheet. See Figure 1-6.

Figure 1-6 ◄
Worksheet
screen after
moving to
different area
of worksheet

row headings
changed

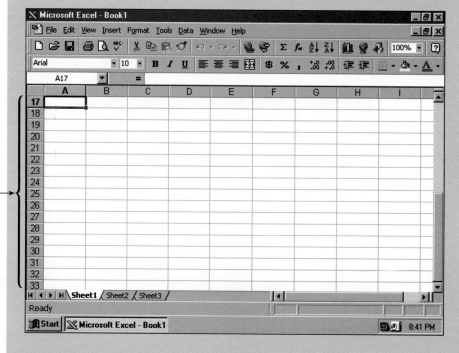

2. Press the **Page Down** key again to move the display down one screen. Notice that the row numbers indicate that you have moved to a different area of the worksheet.

3. Press the **Page Up** key to move the display up one screen. The active cell is now cell A17 (the active cell on your screen may be different).

4. Click the **vertical scroll bar arrow** until row 12 is visible. Notice that the active cell is still A17 (the active cell on your screen may be different). Using the scroll bar changes the portion of the screen you can view without changing the active cell.

5. Click cell **C12** to make it the active cell.

6. Click the blank area above the vertical scroll box to move up a full screen.

7. Click the blank area below the vertical scroll box to move down a full screen.

8. Click the **scroll box** and drag it to the top of the scroll area to again change the area of the screen you're viewing. Notice that the ScrollTip appears telling you where you will scroll to.

9. Click cell **E6** to make it the active cell.

As you know, a workbook can consist of one or more worksheets. Excel makes it easy to switch between them. Next, try moving from worksheet to worksheet.

Excel

Navigating in a Workbook

The sheet tabs let you move quickly between the different sheets in a workbook. If you can see the tab of the sheet you want, click the tab to activate the worksheet. You can also use the sheet tab scroll buttons to see sheet tabs hidden from view. Figure 1-7 describes the four tab scrolling buttons and their effects.

Figure 1-7 ◀
Sheet tab
scrolling
buttons

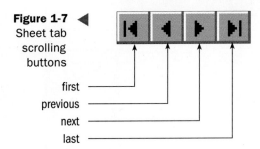

first ———
previous ———
next ———
last ———

Next, try moving to a new sheet.

To move to Sheet2:

> **1.** Click the **Sheet2** tab. Sheet2, which is blank, appears in the worksheet window. Notice that the Sheet2 sheet tab is white and the name is bold, which means that Sheet2 is now the active sheet. Cell A1 is the active cell in Sheet2.
>
> **2.** Click the **Sheet3** tab to make it the active sheet.
>
> **3.** Click the **Sheet1** tab to make it the active sheet. Notice that cell E6 is the active cell.

Now that you have some basic skills navigating a worksheet and workbook, you can begin working with Mike to complete the golf site selection worksheet.

Opening a Workbook

When you want to use a workbook that you previously created, you must first open it. Opening a workbook transfers a copy of the workbook file from the hard drive or 3½-inch disk to the random access memory (RAM) of your computer and displays it on your screen. When the workbook is open, the file is both in RAM and on the disk.

After you open a workbook, you can view, edit, print, or save it again on your disk.

REFERENCE
window

OPENING A WORKBOOK

- Click the Open button on the Standard toolbar (or click File, and then click Open).
- Make sure the Look in list box displays the name of the folder containing the workbook you want to open.
- Click the name of the workbook you want to open.
- Click Open.

Mike created a workbook to help the site selection team evaluate the four potential locations for the golf course. The workbook, Inwood, is on your Student Disk.

To open an existing workbook:

> **1.** Place your Excel Student Disk in the appropriate drive.
>
> **TROUBLE?** If you don't have a Student Disk, you need to get one before you can proceed. Your instructor or technical support person will either give you one or ask you to make your own by following the instructions on the "Read This Before You Begin" page before this tutorial. See your instructor or technical support person for information.

2. Click the **Open** button 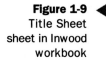 on the Standard toolbar. The Open File dialog box opens. See Figure 1-8.

Figure 1-8 ◀
Open dialog
box

names and files
specified here
(yours may differ)

click here to
specify drive

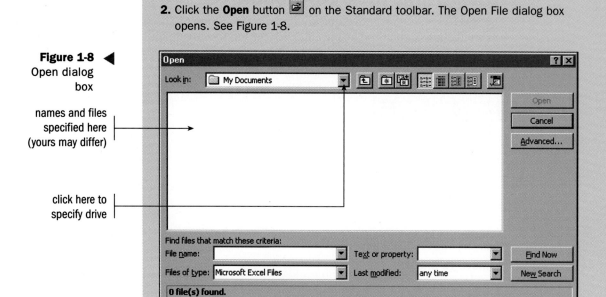

3. Click the **Look in** list arrow to display the list of available drives. Locate the drive containing your Student Disk. In this text, we assume your Student Disk is a 3½-inch floppy in drive A.

4. Click the drive that contains your Student Disk. A list of documents and folders on your Student Disk appears in the list box.

5. In the list of document and folder names, double-click **Tutorial.01** to display that folder in the Look in list box, then click **Inwood**.

6. Click the **Open** button. (You could also double-click the filename to open the file.) The Inwood workbook opens and the first sheet in the workbook, Title Sheet, appears. See Figure 1-9.

TROUBLE? If you do not see Inwood listed, use the scroll bar to see additional names.

Figure 1-9 ◀
Title Sheet
sheet in Inwood
workbook

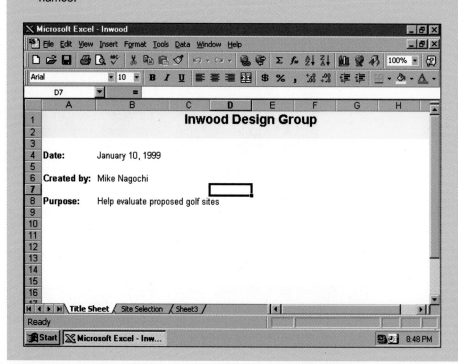

Layout of the Inwood Workbook

The first worksheet, Title Sheet, contains information about the workbook. The Title Sheet shows who created the workbook, the date when it was created, and its purpose.

Mike explains that whenever he creates a new workbook he makes sure he documents it carefully. This information is especially useful if he returns to a workbook after a long period of time (or if a new user opens it) because it provides a quick review of the workbook's purpose.

After reviewing the Title Sheet, Mike moves to the Site Selection worksheet.

To move to the Site Selection worksheet:

1. Click the **Site Selection** sheet tab to display the worksheet Mike is preparing for the site selection team. See Figure 1-10.

Figure 1-10 ◄
Site Selection
worksheet

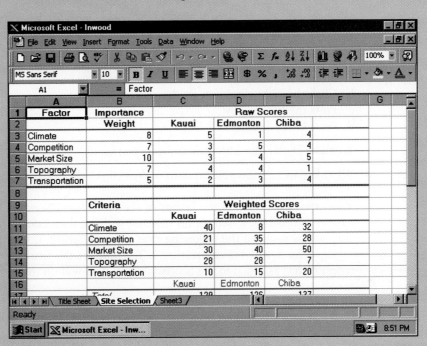

Mike explains the general layout of the Site Selection worksheet to you. He reminds you that to this point he has only entered data for three of the four sites. He will provide the missing Scottsdale information to you. Cells C2 through E2 list three of the four sites under consideration for which he has data. Cells A3 through A7 contain the five factors on which the team's decision will be based: Climate, Competition, Market Size, Topography, and Transportation. They assign scores for climate, competition, market size, topography, and transportation to each location. The team uses a scale of 1 to 5 to assign a raw score for each factor. Higher raw scores indicate strength; lower raw scores indicate weakness. Cells C3 through E7 contain the raw scores for the first three locations. For example, the raw score for Kauai's climate is 5; the two other locations have scores of 1 and 4, so Kauai, with its warm, sunny days all year, has the best climate for the golf course of the three sites visited so far. Edmonton, on the other hand, has cold weather and only received a climate raw score of 1.

The raw scores, however, do not provide enough information for the team to make a decision. Some factors are more important to the success of the golf course than others. The team members assigned an *importance weight* to each factor according to their knowledge of what factors contribute most to the success of a golf course. The importance weights are on a scale from 1 to 10, with 10 being most important. Mike entered the weights in cells B3 through B7. Market size, weighted 10, is the most important factor. The team believes the least important factor is transportation, so transportation is assigned a lower weight. Climate is important but the team considers market size most important. Therefore, they do not use the raw scores to make a final decision. Instead, they multiply each raw score by its importance weight to produce a weighted score. Which of the three sites already visited has the highest weighted score for any factor? If you look at the scores in cells C11 through E15, you see that Chiba's score of 50 for market size is the highest weighted score for any factor.

Cells C17 through E17 contain the total weighted scores for the three locations. With the current weighting and raw scores, Chiba is the most promising site, with a total score of 137.

Quick Check

1. A(n) _____ is the rectangular area where a column and a row intersect.

2. When you _____ a workbook, the computer copies it from your disk into RAM.

3. The cell reference _____ refers to the intersection of the fourth column and the second row.

4. To move the worksheet to the right one column:
   a. Press the Enter key
   b. Click the right arrow on the horizontal scroll bar
   c. Press the Escape key
   d. Press Ctrl + Home

5. To make Sheet2 the active worksheet, you would _____.

6. What key or keys do you press to make cell A1 the active cell?

You have now reviewed the layout of the worksheet. Now, Mike wants you to enter the data on Scottsdale. Based on his meeting with local investors and a visit to the Scottsdale site, he has assigned the following raw scores: Climate 5, Competition 2, Market Size 4, Topography 3, and Transportation 3. To complete the worksheet, you must enter the raw scores he has assigned to the Scottsdale site. You will do this in the next session.

SESSION

1.2

In this session you will learn how to enter text, values, formulas, and functions into a worksheet. You will use this data to perform what-if analysis using a worksheet. You'll also correct mistakes, and use the online Help system to determine how to clear the contents of cells. Finally, you'll learn how to print a worksheet, and how to close a worksheet and exit Excel.

Text, Values, Formulas, and Functions

As you have now observed, an Excel workbook can hold one or more worksheets, each containing a grid of 256 columns and 65,536 rows. The rectangular areas at the intersections of each column and row are called cells. A cell can contain a value, text, or a formula. To understand how the spreadsheet program works, you need to understand how Excel manipulates text, values, formulas, and functions.

Text

Text entries include any combination of letters, symbols, numbers, and spaces. Although text is sometimes used as data, it is more often used to describe the data contained in a worksheet. Text is often used to label columns and rows in a worksheet. For example, a projected monthly income statement contains the months of the year as column headings and income and expense categories as row labels. To enter text in a worksheet, you select the cell in which you want to enter the text by clicking the cell to select it, then typing the text. Excel automatically aligns the text on the left when it is displayed in a cell.

Mike's Site Selection worksheet contains a number of column heading labels. You need to enter the label for Scottsdale in the Raw Scores and Weighted Scores sections of the worksheet.

To enter a text label:

1. If you took a break after the last session, make sure Excel is running and make sure the Site Selection worksheet of the Inwood workbook is displayed.

2. Click cell **F2** to make it the active cell.

3. Type **Scottsdale**, then press the **Enter** key.

    TROUBLE? If you make a mistake while typing, you can correct the error with the Backspace key. If you realize you made an error after you press the Enter key, retype the entry by repeating Steps 2 and 3.

4. Click cell **F10** and type **S**. Excel completes the entry for you based on the entries already in the column. If your data involves repetitious text, this feature, known as **AutoComplete,** can make your data entry go more quickly.

5. Press the **Enter** key to complete the entry.

6. Click cell **F16**, type **S**, and press the **Enter** key to accept Scottsdale as the entry in the cell. See Figure 1-11.

Figure 1-11 ◄
Worksheet after text entered

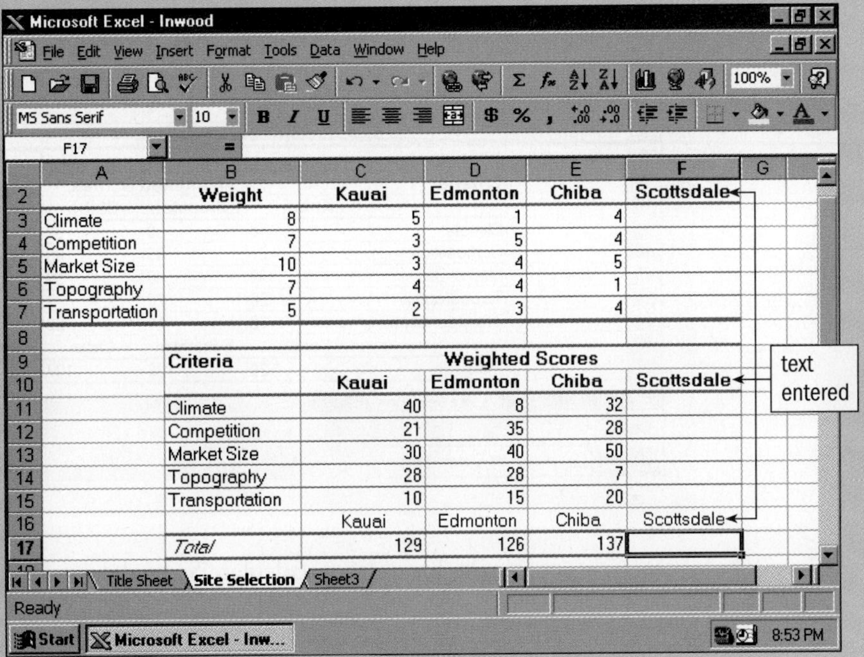

Next, you need to enter the raw scores Mike assigned to Scottsdale.

Values

Values are numbers that represent a quantity of some type: the number of units in inventory, stock price, an exam score, and so on. Examples of values are 378, 25.2, and -55. Values can also be dates (11/29/99) and times (4:40:31). As you type information in a cell, Excel determines whether the characters you're typing can be used as values. For example, if you type 456, Excel recognizes it as a value and it is right-justified when displayed in the cell. On the other hand, Excel treats some data commonly referred to as "numbers" as text. For example, Excel treats a telephone number (1-800-227-1240) or a social security number (372-70-9654) as text that cannot be used for calculations.

You need to enter the raw scores for Scottsdale.

To enter a value:

1. If necessary, click the scroll arrow so row 2 is visible. Click cell **F3**, type **5** and then press the **Enter** key. The cell pointer moves to cell F4.

2. With the cell pointer in cell F4, type **2** and press the **Enter** key.

3. Enter the value **4** for Market Size in cell F5, the value **3** for Topography in cell F6, and the value **3** for Transportation in cell F7. See Figure 1-12.

Figure 1-12 ◀
Worksheet
after numbers
entered

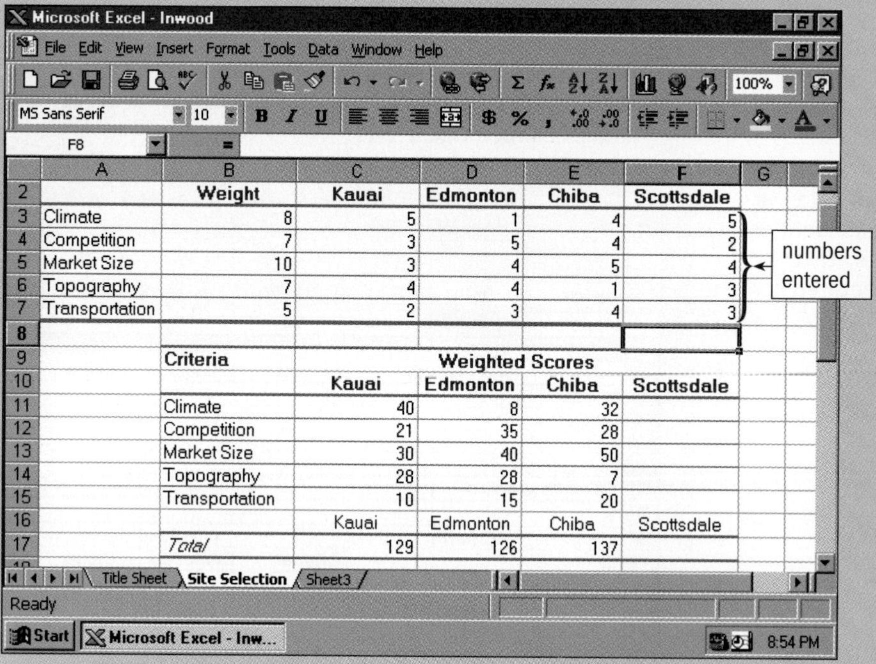

Next, you enter the formulas to calculate Scottsdale's weighted score in each category.

Formulas

When you need to perform a calculation in Excel you use a formula. A **formula** is the arithmetic used to calculate values displayed in a worksheet. You can take advantage of the power of Excel by using formulas in worksheets. If you change one number in a worksheet, Excel recalculates any formula affected by the change.

An Excel formula always begins with an equal sign (=). Formulas are created by combining numbers, cell references, arithmetic operators, and/or functions. An **arithmetic operator** indicates the desired arithmetic operations. Figure 1-13 shows the arithmetic operators used in Excel.

Figure 1-13
Arithmetic
operators used
in formulas

Arithmetic Operation	Arithmetic Operator	Example	Description
Addition	+	=10+A5	Adds 10 to the value in cell A5
Subtraction	–	=C9–B9	Subtracts the value in cell B9 from the value in cell C9
Multiplication	*	=C9*B9	Multiplies the value in cell B9 by the value in cell C9
Division	/	=C9/B9	Divides the value in cell C9 by the value in cell B9
Exponentiation	^	=10^B5	Raises 10 to the value stored in cell B5

The result of the formula is displayed in the cell where you entered the formula. To view the formula that has been entered in a cell, you must first select the cell, then look at the formula bar.

REFERENCE window

ENTERING A FORMULA

- Click the cell where you want the result to appear.
- Type = and then type the rest of the formula.
- For formulas that include cell references, such as B2 or D78, you can type the cell reference or you can use the mouse or arrow keys to select each cell.
- When the formula is complete, press the Enter key.

You need to enter the formulas to compute the weighted scores for the Scottsdale site. The formula multiples the raw score for a factor by the importance weight assigned to the factor. Figure 1-14 displays the formulas you need to enter into the worksheet.

Figure 1-14
Formula to
calculate
Scottsdale's
weighted score

Cell	Formula	Explanation
F11	=B3*F3	Multiplies importance weight by raw score for climate
F12	=B4*F4	Multiplies importance weight by raw score for competition
F13	=B5*F5	Multiplies importance weight by raw score for market size
F14	=B6*F6	Multiplies importance weight by raw score for topography
F15	=B7*F7	Multiplies importance weight by raw score for transportation

To enter the formula to calculate each weighted score for the Scottsdale site:

1. Click cell **F11** to make it the active cell. Type **=B3*F3** to multiply the weight assigned to the climate category by the raw score assigned to Scottsdale for the climate category. Press the **Enter** key. The value 40 is displayed in cell F11.

   TROUBLE? If you make a mistake while typing, you can correct the error with the Backspace key. If you realize you made an error after you press the Enter key, repeat Step 1 to retype the entry.

2. Click cell **F12**, type **=B4*F4**, and then press the **Enter** key. This formula multiplies the weight assigned to competition (the contents of cell B4) by Scottsdale's raw score for competition (cell F4). The value 14 is displayed.

3. Enter the remaining formulas from Figure 1-14 into cells F13, F14, and F15. When completed, your worksheet will look like Figure 1-15.

Figure 1-15 ◀
Worksheet after entering formulas to calculate weighted score

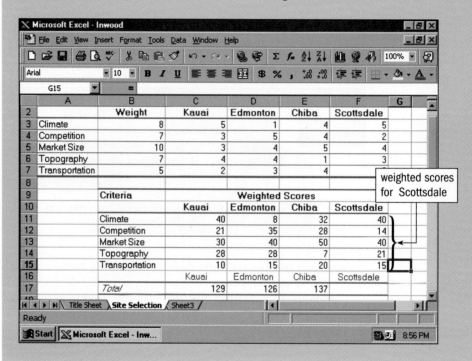

You now have to enter the formula to calculate the total weighted score for Scottsdale into the worksheet. You can use the formula *=F11+F12+F13+F14+F15* to calculate the total score for the Scottsdale site. As an alternative, you can use a function to streamline this long formula.

Functions

A **function** is a special prewritten formula that's a shortcut for commonly used calculations. For example, the SUM function is a shortcut for entering formulas that total values in rows or columns. You can use the SUM function to create the formula =SUM(F11:F15) instead of typing the longer =F11+F12+F13+F14+F15. The SUM function in this example adds the range F11 through F15. A **range** can be a single cell or a rectangular block of cells, often rows or columns. The range reference in the function SUM(F11:F15) refers to the rectangular block of cells beginning at F11 and ending at F15. Figure 1-16 shows several examples of ranges.

Figure 1-16 ◀
Examples of
ranges

range D4:I4

range B3:B9

range D14:D14

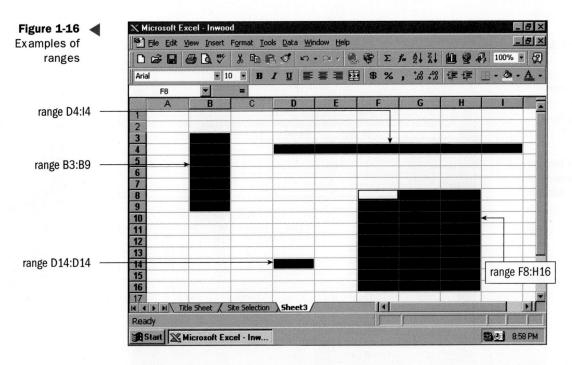

range F8:H16

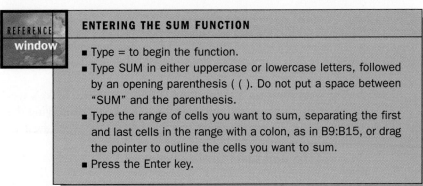

ENTERING THE SUM FUNCTION

- Type = to begin the function.
- Type SUM in either uppercase or lowercase letters, followed by an opening parenthesis (( ). Do not put a space between "SUM" and the parenthesis.
- Type the range of cells you want to sum, separating the first and last cells in the range with a colon, as in B9:B15, or drag the pointer to outline the cells you want to sum.
- Press the Enter key.

You use the SUM function to compute the total score for the Scottsdale site.

To enter the formula using a function:

1. Click cell **F17** to make it the active cell.

2. Type **=SUM(F11:F15)**. Notice that the formula appears in the cell and the formula bar as you enter it. See Figure 1-17.

Figure 1-17 ◄
Viewing
the SUM
function before
completing
the entry

SUM function
appears in
formula bar

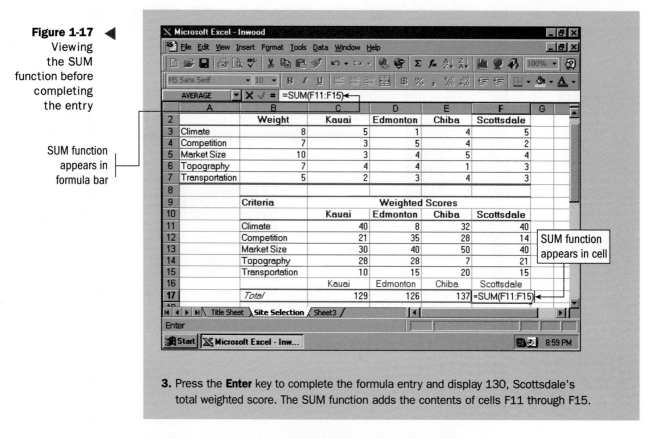

3. Press the **Enter** key to complete the formula entry and display 130, Scottsdale's total weighted score. The SUM function adds the contents of cells F11 through F15.

The worksheet for site selection is now complete. Mike's worksheet contains columns of information about the site selection and a chart displaying the weighted scores for each potential site. To see the chart you must scroll the worksheet.

To scroll the worksheet to view the chart:

1. Click the **scroll arrow** button on the vertical scroll bar until the section of the worksheet containing the chart is displayed. See Figure 1-18.

Figure 1-18 ◄
Scrolling the
worksheet to
view the chart

Chiba is leading site

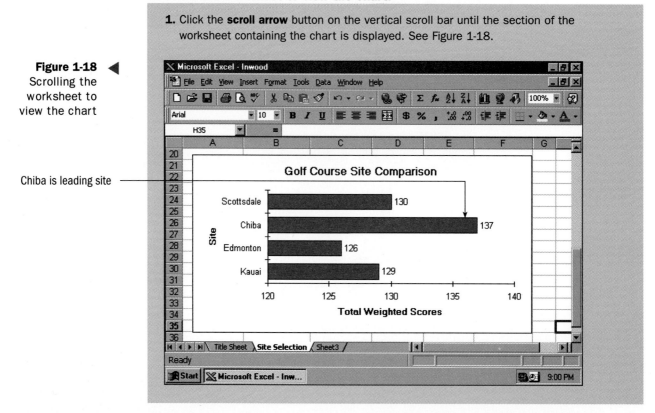

2. After you look at the chart, click and drag the **scroll box** to the top of the vertical scroll bar.

You have completed the worksheet; Mike decides to save it before showing it to the site selection team.

Saving the Workbook

To store a workbook permanently, so you can use it again without having to reenter the data and formulas, you must save it as a file on a disk. When you save a workbook, you copy it from RAM onto your disk. You'll use either the Save or the Save As command. The Save command copies the workbook onto a disk using its current filename. If a version of the file already exists, the new version replaces the old one. The Save As command asks for a filename before copying the workbook onto a disk. When you enter a new filename, you save the current file under that new name. The previous version of the file remains on the disk under its original name.

As a general rule, use the Save As command the first time you save a file or whenever you modify a file and want to save both the old and new versions. Use the Save command when you modify a file and want to save only the current version.

It is a good idea to save your file often. That way, if the power goes out or the computer stops working, you're less likely to lose your work. Because you use the Save command frequently, the Standard toolbar has a Save button , a single mouse-click shortcut for saving your workbook.

REFERENCE window	**SAVING A WORKBOOK WITH A NEW FILENAME**
	■ Click File and then click Save As.
	■ Change the workbook name as necessary.
	■ Make sure the Save in box displays the folder in which you want to save your workbook.
	■ Click the Save button.

Mike's workbook is named Inwood. On your screen is a version of Inwood that you modified during this work session. Save the modified workbook under the new name Inwood 2. This way if you want to start the tutorial from the beginning, you can open the Inwood file and start over.

To save the modified workbook under a new name:

1. Click **File** on the menu bar, and then click **Save As**. The Save As dialog box opens with the current workbook name in the File name text box.

2. Click at the end of the current workbook name, press the **spacebar**, and then type **2**. *(Do not press the Enter key.)*

Before you proceed, check the other dialog box specifications to ensure that you save the workbook on your Student Disk.

3. If necessary, click the **Save in** list arrow to display the list of available drives and folders. Click **Tutorial.01**.

4. Confirm that the Save as type text box specifies "Microsoft Excel Workbook."

5. When your Save As dialog box looks like the one in Figure 1-19, click the **Save** button to close the dialog box and save the workbook. Notice that the new workbook name, Inwood 2, now appears in the title bar.

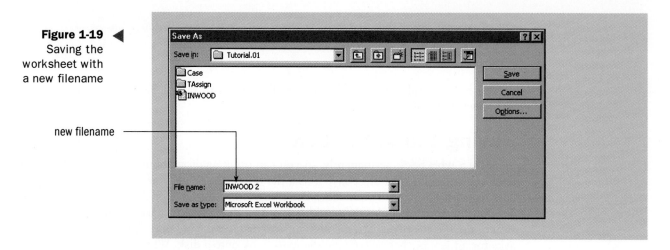

Figure 1-19
Saving the
worksheet with
a new filename

new filename

You now have two versions of the workbook: the original file—Inwood—and the modified workbook—Inwood 2.

Changing Values and Observing Results

The worksheet for site selection is now complete. Mike is ready to show it to the group. As the team examines the worksheet, you ask if the raw scores take into account recent news that a competing design group has announced plans to build a $325-million golf resort just 10 miles away from Inwood's proposed site in Chiba. Mike admits that he assigned the values before the announcement, so the raw scores do not reflect the increased competition in the Chiba market. You suggest revising the raw score for the competition factor to reflect this market change in Chiba.

When you change a value in a worksheet, Excel recalculates the worksheet and displays updated results. The recalculation feature makes Excel an extremely useful decision-making tool because it lets you quickly and easily factor in changing conditions. When you revise the contents of one or more cells in a worksheet and observe the effect this change has on all the other cells, you are performing a **what-if analysis**. In effect, you are saying, what if I change the value assigned to this factor? What effect will it have on the outcomes in the worksheet?

Since another development group has announced plans to construct a new golf course in the Chiba area, the team decides to lower Chiba's competition raw score from 4 to 2.

To change Chiba's competition raw score from 4 to 2:

1. Click cell **E4**. The black border around cell E4 indicates that it is the active cell. The current value of cell E4 is 4.

2. Type **2**. Notice that 2 appears in the cell and in the formula bar, along with a formula palette of three new buttons. The buttons shown in Figure 1-20—the Cancel button ⊠, the Enter button ☑, and the Edit Formula button ▣—offer alternatives for canceling, entering, and editing data and formulas.

Excel

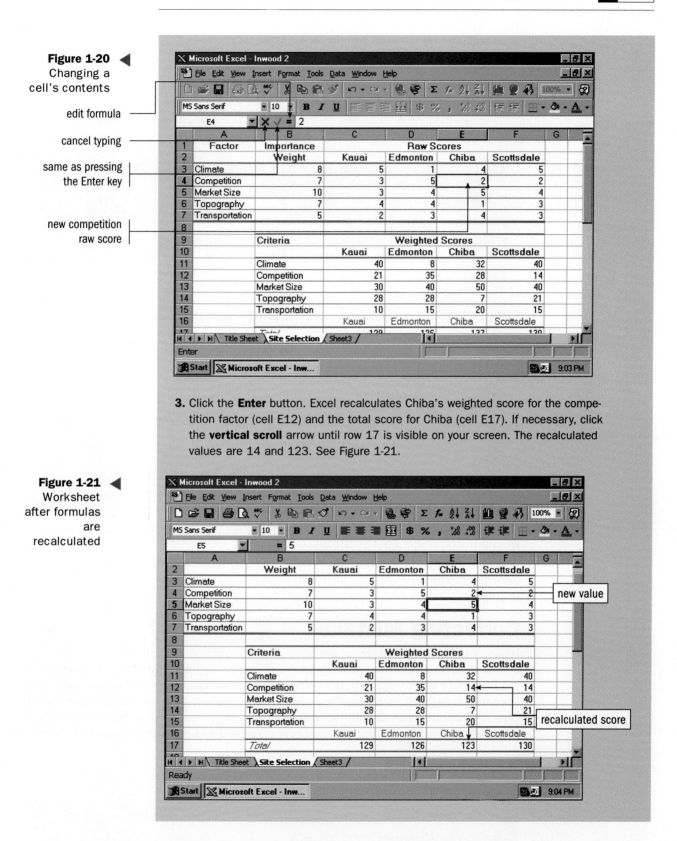

Figure 1-20 ◀
Changing a
cell's contents

edit formula

cancel typing

same as pressing
the Enter key

new competition
raw score

3. Click the **Enter** button. Excel recalculates Chiba's weighted score for the competition factor (cell E12) and the total score for Chiba (cell E17). If necessary, click the **vertical scroll** arrow until row 17 is visible on your screen. The recalculated values are 14 and 123. See Figure 1-21.

Figure 1-21 ◀
Worksheet
after formulas
are
recalculated

The team takes another look at the total weighted scores in row 17. Scottsdale is now the top-ranking site, with a total weighted score of 130. Chiba's total weighted score is now 123.

As the team continues to discuss the worksheet, several members express concern over the importance weight used for transportation. In the current worksheet, transportation is weighted 5 (cell B7). You remember that the group agreed to use an importance weight of 2 at a previous meeting. You ask Mike to change the importance weight for transportation.

To change the importance weight for transportation:

1. Click cell **B7** to make it the active cell.
2. Type **2** and press the **Enter** key. Cell B7 now contains the value 2 instead of 5. Cell B8 becomes the active cell. See Figure 1-22. Notice that the weighted scores for transportation (row 15) and the total weighted scores for each site (row 17) have all changed.

Figure 1-22 Worksheet after change made to the transportation importance weight

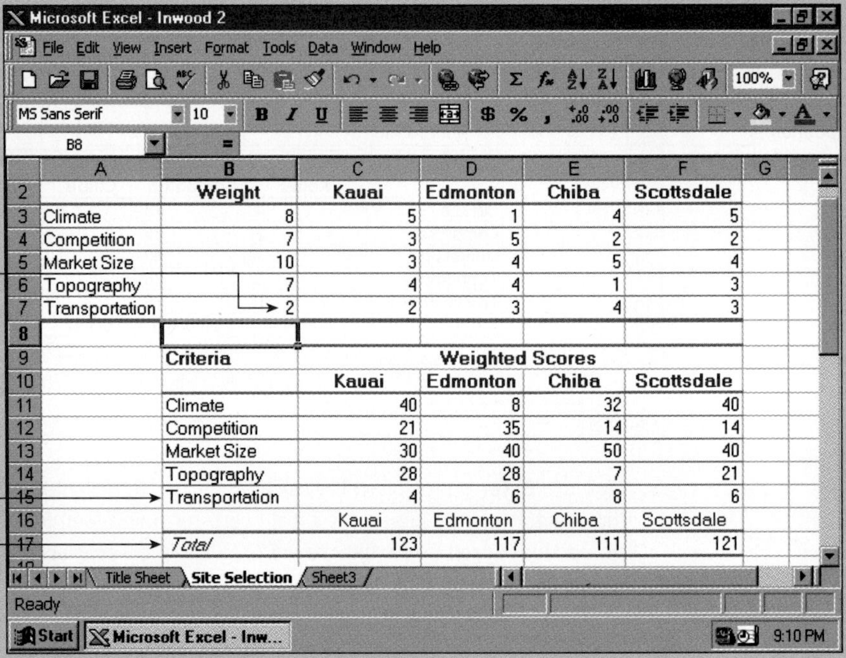
Microsoft Excel - Inwood 2
File Edit View Insert Format Tools Data Window Help
MS Sans Serif
10
100%
B8
A B C D E F G
2 Weight Kauai Edmonton Chiba Scottsdale
3 Climate 8 5 1 4 5
4 Competition 7 3 5 2 2
5 Market Size 10 3 4 5 4
6 Topography 7 4 4 1 3
7 Transportation 2 2 3 4 3
8
9 Criteria Weighted Scores
10 Kauai Edmonton Chiba Scottsdale
11 Climate 40 8 32 40
12 Competition 21 35 14 14
13 Market Size 30 40 50 40
14 Topography 28 28 7 21
15 Transportation 4 6 8 6
16 Kauai Edmonton Chiba Scottsdale
17 Total 123 117 111 121
Title Sheet Site Selection Sheet3
Ready
Start Microsoft Excel - Inw...
9:10 PM

new value

all transportation scores recalculated

all total scores recalculated

The change in the transportation importance weight puts Kauai ahead as the most favorable site, with a total weighted score of 123.

As you enter and edit a worksheet, there are many data entry errors that can occur. The most commonly made mistake on a worksheet is a typing error. Typing mistakes are easy to correct.

Correcting Mistakes

It is easy to correct a mistake as you are typing information in a cell, before you press the Enter key. If you need to correct a mistake as you are typing information in a cell, press the Backspace key to back up and delete one or more characters. When you are typing information in a cell, don't use the cursor arrow keys to edit because they move the cell pointer to another cell. One of the team members suggests changing the label "Criteria" in cell B9 to "Factors." The team members agree and you make the change to the cell.

To correct a mistake as you type:

1. Click cell **B9** to make it the active cell.
2. Type **Fak**, intentionally making an error, but don't press the Enter key.
3. Press the **Backspace** key to delete "k."
4. Type **ctors** and press the **Enter** key.

Excel

Now the word "Factors" is in cell B9. Mike suggests changing "Factors" to "Factor." The team agrees. To change a cell's contents after you press the Enter key, you use a different method. Double-clicking a cell or pressing the F2 key puts Excel into Edit mode, which lets you use the Backspace key, the ← and → keys, and the mouse to change the text in the formula bar.

REFERENCE window

CORRECTING MISTAKES USING EDIT MODE

- Double-click the cell you want to edit to begin Edit mode and display the contents of the cell in the formula bar (or click the cell you want to edit, then press F2).
- Use Backspace, Delete, ←, →, or the mouse to edit the cell's contents either in the cell or in the formula bar.
- Press the Enter key when you finish editing.

You use Edit mode to change "Factors" to "Factor" in cell B9.

To change the word "Factors" to "Factor" in cell B9:

1. Double-click cell **B9** to begin Edit mode. Note that "Edit" appears in the status bar, reminding you that Excel is currently in Edit mode.

2. Press the **End** key if necessary to move the cursor to the right of the word "Factors," then press the **Backspace** key to delete the "s."

3. Press the **Enter** key to complete the edit.

You ask if the team is ready to recommend a site. Mike believes that based on the best information they have, Kauai should be the recommended site and Scottsdale the alternative site. You ask for a vote, and the team unanimously agrees with Mike's recommendation.

Mike wants to have complete documentation to accompany the team's written recommendation to management, so he wants to print the worksheet.

As he reviews the worksheet one last time, he thinks that the labels in cells C16 through F16 (Kauai, Edmonton, Chiba, Scottsdale) are unnecessary and decides he wants you to delete them before printing the worksheet. You ask how you delete the contents of a cell or a group of cells. Mike is not sure, so he suggests using the Excel Help system to find the answer.

Getting Help

If you don't know how to perform a task or forget how to carry out a particular task, Excel provides an extensive Help system. The Excel Help system provides the same options as the Help system in other Windows programs—the Help Contents, the Help Index, and the Find feature. The Excel Help system also provides additional ways to get help as you work. One way to get help is to use the Office Assistant, which you may have seen on your screen when you first started Excel, and which you hid earlier in this tutorial. The Office Assistant, an animated object, pops up on the screen when you click the Office Assistant button on the Standard toolbar. The Office Assistant answers questions, offers tips, and provides help for a variety of Excel features. In addition to the Office Assistant, Figure 1-23 identifies several other ways you can get help.

Figure 1-23 ◀
Alternative ways
to get help

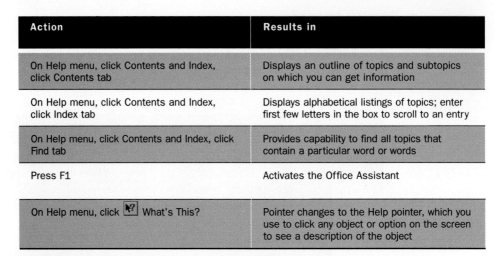

Action	Results in
On Help menu, click Contents and Index, click Contents tab	Displays an outline of topics and subtopics on which you can get information
On Help menu, click Contents and Index, click Index tab	Displays alphabetical listings of topics; enter first few letters in the box to scroll to an entry
On Help menu, click Contents and Index, click Find tab	Provides capability to find all topics that contain a particular word or words
Press F1	Activates the Office Assistant
On Help menu, click ▧ What's This?	Pointer changes to the Help pointer, which you use to click any object or option on the screen to see a description of the object

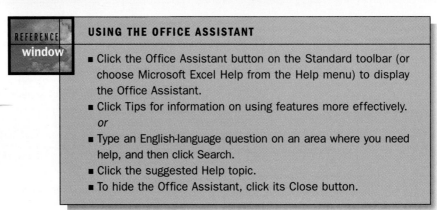

REFERENCE window

USING THE OFFICE ASSISTANT

- Click the Office Assistant button on the Standard toolbar (or choose Microsoft Excel Help from the Help menu) to display the Office Assistant.
- Click Tips for information on using features more effectively.
  or
- Type an English-language question on an area where you need help, and then click Search.
- Click the suggested Help topic.
- To hide the Office Assistant, click its Close button.

Use the Office Assistant to get information on how to clear the contents of cells.

To get Help using the Office Assistant:

1. Click the Office Assistant ▨ button to display an animated object and an information box. See Figure 1-24.

Figure 1-24 ◀
Office
Assistant with
information box

enter question here ——

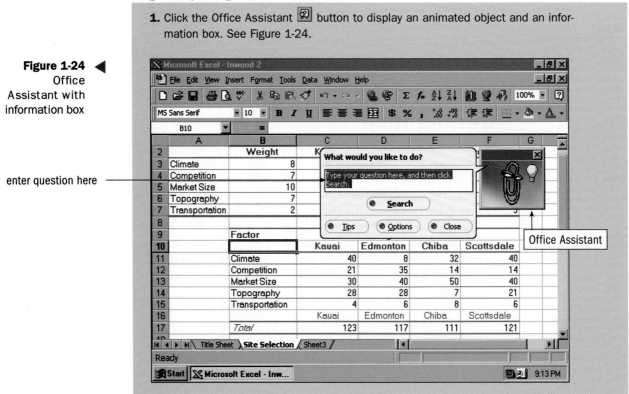

Office Assistant

Excel

The Office Assistant can respond to an English-language question.

2. Type **how do I clear cells**, and then click **Search** to display several possible Help topics. See Figure 1-25.

Figure 1-25 ◄
Office Assistant with several suggested Help topics

click this topic ───

suggested Help topics

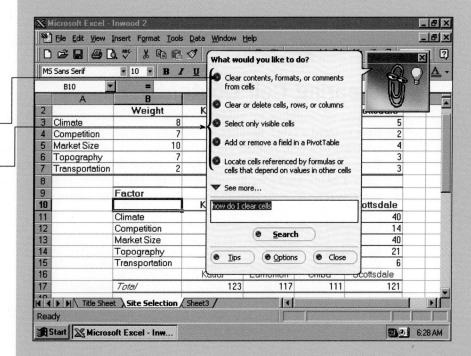

3. Click the first suggestion, **Clear contents, formats, or comments from cells**, to open a How To window on this topic. See Figure 1-26.

Figure 1-26 ◄
How To window on Clear contents, formats, or comments from cells

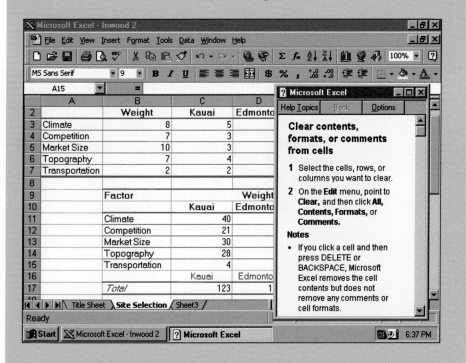

You can print the contents of the How To window, or you can click the Keep Help On Top command from the Options menu to keep the How To window on the screen where you can refer to it as you go through each step.

4. After reviewing the information, click the **Close** button ☒ on the How To window.

5. Click the **Close** button ☒ in the upper-right corner of the Office Assistant to hide the Assistant.

After reviewing the information from the Office Assistant, you are ready to remove the labels from the worksheet.

Clearing Cell Contents

As you are building or modifying your worksheet, you may occasionally find that you have entered a label, number, or formula in a cell that you want to be empty. To erase the contents of a cell, you use either the Delete key or the Clear command on the Edit menu. Removing the contents of a cell is known as clearing a cell. Do not press the spacebar to enter a blank character in an attempt to clear a cell's content. Excel treats a blank character as text, so even though the cell appears to be empty, it is not.

REFERENCE window

CLEARING CELL CONTENTS

- Click the cell you want to clear, or select a range of cells you want to clear.
- Press the Delete key.
  or
- Click Edit, point to Clear, and then click Contents to erase only the contents of a cell, or click All to completely clear the cell contents, formatting, and notes.

You are ready to clear the labels from cells C16 through F16.

To clear the labels from cells C16 through F16:

1. Click cell **C16**. This will be the upper-left corner of the range to clear.

2. Position the cell pointer over cell C16. With the cell pointer the shape of ✛, click and drag the cell pointer to F16 to select the range C16:F16.
If your pointer changes to a crosshair ✛ , or an arrow ⬉ , do not drag the cell pointer to F16, until pointer changes to ✛ . Note that when you select a range, the first cell in that range, cell C16 in this example, remains white and the other cells in the range are highlighted. See Figure 1-27.

Figure 1-27
Highlighted cell
range

highlighted range ────

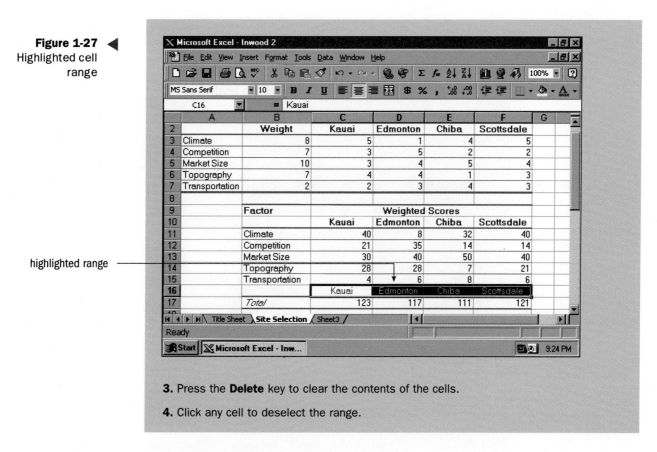

3. Press the **Delete** key to clear the contents of the cells.

4. Click any cell to deselect the range.

Now that you have cleared the unwanted labels from the cells, Mike wants you to print the site selection worksheet.

Printing the Worksheet

You can print an Excel worksheet using either the Print command on the File menu or the Print button on the Standard toolbar. If you use the Print command, Excel displays a dialog box where you can specify which worksheet pages you want to print, the number of copies you want to print, and the print quality (resolution). If you use the Print button, you do not have these options; Excel prints one copy of the entire worksheet using the current print settings.

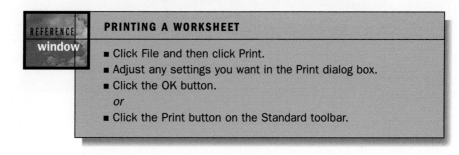

REFERENCE
window

PRINTING A WORKSHEET

- Click File and then click Print.
- Adjust any settings you want in the Print dialog box.
- Click the OK button.
  or
- Click the Print button on the Standard toolbar.

Mike wants a printout of the entire Site Selection worksheet. You decide to select the Print command from the File menu instead of using the Print button so you can check the Print dialog box settings.

To check the print settings and then print the worksheet:

1. Make sure your printer is turned on and contains paper.

2. Click **File** on the menu bar, and then click **Print** to display the Print dialog box. See Figure 1-28.

Figure 1-28 ◀
Print dialog box

identifies printer (your entry may be different)

prints selected range in worksheet

prints active sheet

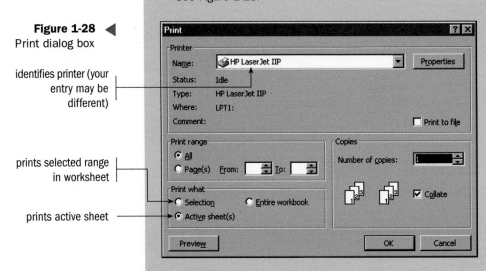

Now you need to select what to print. You could print the complete workbook, which would be the Title Sheet and the Site Selection sheet. To do this, you would click the Entire workbook option button. You could also choose to print just a portion of a worksheet. For example, to print only the weighted scores data of the Site Selection worksheet, first select this range with your mouse pointer, and then select the Selection option button in the Print dialog box. In this case, Mike needs just the Site Selection worksheet.

3. If necessary, click the **Active sheet(s)** option button in the Print what section of the dialog box to print just the Site Selection worksheet, and not the Title Sheet.

4. Make sure "1" appears in the Number of copies text box, as Mike only needs to print one copy of the worksheet.

5. Click the **OK** button to print the worksheet. See Figure 1-29.

   TROUBLE? If the worksheet does not print, see your technical support person for help.

Figure 1-29 ◀
Printed
worksheet

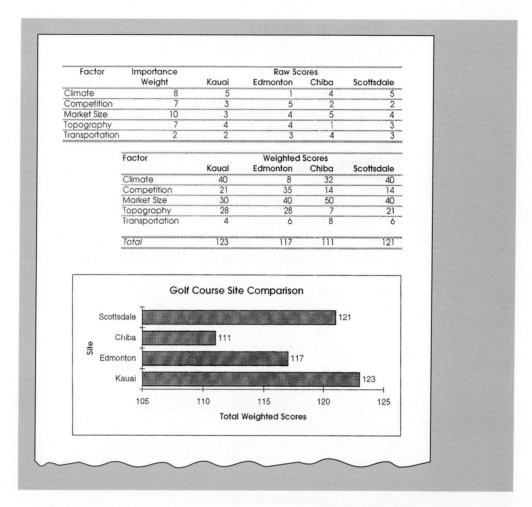

Factor	Importance Weight	Raw Scores			
		Kauai	Edmonton	Chiba	Scottsdale
Climate	8	5	1	4	5
Competition	7	3	5	2	2
Market Size	10	3	4	5	4
Topography	7	4	4	1	3
Transportation	2	2	3	4	3

Factor	Weighted Scores			
	Kauai	Edmonton	Chiba	Scottsdale
Climate	40	8	32	40
Competition	21	35	14	14
Market Size	30	40	50	40
Topography	28	28	7	21
Transportation	4	6	8	6
Total	123	117	111	121

Golf Course Site Comparison

Scottsdale 121
Chiba 111
Edmonton 117
Kauai 123

Site

105   110   115   120   125
Total Weighted Scores

Mike volunteers to put together the report with the team's final recommendation, and the meeting adjourns. You and Mike are finished working with the worksheet and are ready to close the workbook.

Closing the Workbook

Closing a workbook removes it from the screen. If a workbook contains changes that have not been saved, Excel asks if you want to save your modified worksheet before closing the workbook. You can now close the workbook.

To close the Inwood 2 workbook:

1. Click **File** on the menu bar, and then click **Close**. A dialog box displays the message "Do you want to save the changes you made to 'INWOOD 2'?"

2. Click the **Yes** button to save the Inwood 2 workbook before closing it.

The Excel window stays open so you can open or create another workbook. You do not want to, so your next step is to exit Excel.

Exiting Excel

To exit Excel, you can click the Close button on the title bar, or you can use the Exit command on the File menu.

To exit Excel:

1. Click the Close button ☒ on the title bar. Excel closes and you return to the Windows desktop.

Quick Check

1 The formula =SUM(D1:K1) adds how many cells? Write an equivalent formula without using the SUM function.

2 What cells are included in the range B4:D6?

3 Indicate whether Excel treats the following cell entries as a value, text, or a formula:

 a. Profit

 b. 11/09/95

 c. 123

 d. =B9*225

 e. 1-800-227-1240

 f. =SUM(C1:C10)

 g. 123 N. First St.

4 To print the entire worksheet, you select the _____ option button from the _____ dialog box.

5 To print a copy of your worksheet, you use the _____ command on the _____ menu.

6 You can get Excel Help in any of the following ways except:

 a. clicking Help on the menu bar

 b. clicking the Help button on the Standard toolbar

 c. closing the program window

 d. pressing the F1 key

7 Why do you need to save a worksheet? What command do you use to save the worksheet?

8 What key do you press to clear the contents of a cell from a worksheet?

9 Explain the term *what-if analysis*.

The Inwood site selection team has completed its work. Mike's worksheet helped the team analyze the data and recommend Kauai as the best site for Inwood's next golf course. Although the Japanese market was a strong factor in favor of locating the course in Japan's Chiba Prefecture, the mountainous terrain and competition from nearby courses reduced the site's desirability.

Tutorial Assignments

The other company that had planned a golf course in Chiba, Japan, has run into financial difficulties. Rumors are that the project may be canceled. A copy of the final Inwood Design team workbook is on your Student Disk. Do the Tutorial Assignments to change this worksheet to show the effect of the other project's cancellation on your site selection.

 1. If necessary, start Excel and make sure your Student Disk is in the appropriate disk drive.
 Open the Inwood 3 file in the TAssign folder for Tutorial 1 on your Student Disk.

 2. Use the Save As command to save the workbook as Inwood4 in the TAssign folder for Tutorial 1. That way you won't change the original workbook.

 3. In the Inwood4 worksheet, change the competition raw score for Chiba from 2 to 3. What site is ranked first?

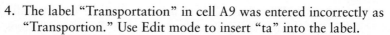

4. The label "Transportation" in cell A9 was entered incorrectly as "Transportion." Use Edit mode to insert "ta" into the label.

5. Save the worksheet.

6. Print the worksheet.

7. Use the Contents and Index command on the Help menu to access the Help Topics dialog box. From the Contents tab, learn how to insert an additional worksheet into your workbook. (*Hint*: Choose Working with workbook and worksheets topic, then managing worksheets.) Write the steps to insert a worksheet.

8. Use the Office Assistant to learn how to delete a sheet from a workbook. Write the steps to delete a sheet.

9. Enter the text "Scores if the competing project in Chiba, Japan, is canceled" in cell A1.

10. Remove the raw scores for Chiba, cells E5 through E9. Print the worksheet.

11. Use the Index command on the Help menu to learn about the AutoCalculate feature. Write a brief explanation of this feature.

12. You are considering dropping transportation as a factor in the site selection decision. Use AutoCalculate to arrive at a revised total weighted score for each of the three remaining sites. Write the response.

13. Print the worksheet data without the chart. (*Hint*: Select the worksheet data before checking out the options in the Print dialog box.)

14. Use the What's This button 【?】. Learn more about the following Excel window components:
    a. Name box
    b. Sheet tabs
    c. Tip Wizard
    (*Hint*: Click 【?】, then click each item with the Help pointer.)

15. Close the workbook and exit Excel without saving the changes.

Case Problems

1. Market Share Analysis at Aldon Industries Helen Shalala is assistant to the regional director for Aldon Industries, a manufacturer of corporate voice mail systems. Helen has analyzed the market share of the top vendors with installations in the region. She's on her way to a meeting with the marketing staff where she will use her worksheet to plan a new marketing campaign. Help Helen and her team evaluate the options and plan the best advertising campaign for Aldon Industries. Write your responses to questions 4 through 10.

1. If necessary, start Excel and make sure your Student Disk is in the appropriate disk drive.

2. Open the workbook Aldon in the Case folder for Tutorial 1.

3. Use the Save As command to save the workbook as Aldon 2 in the Case folder for Tutorial 1. That way you won't change the original workbook for this case.

4. Take a moment to look over the Market Share worksheet. Do the following ranges contain text, values, or formulas?
    a. B13:G13
    b. C3:C10
    c. A3:A10
    d. G3:G10

5. What is Aldon Industries' overall market share?

6. Examine the worksheet to determine in which state Aldon Industries has the highest market share.

7. Which company leads the overall market?

8. What is Aldon Industries' overall ranking in total market share (1st, 2nd, 3rd, etc.)?

9. Which companies rank ahead of Aldon Industries in total market share?

10. What formula was used to calculate Total Installations in Illinois? Develop an alternative formula to calculate Total Installations in Illinois without using the SUM function.

11. Save and print the worksheet.

2. Selecting a Hospital Laboratory Computer System for Bridgeport Medical Center David Choi is on the Laboratory Computer Selection Committee for the Bridgeport Medical Center. After an extensive search, the committee has identified three vendors whose products appear to meet its needs. The Selection Committee has prepared an Excel worksheet to help evaluate the three potential vendors' strengths and weaknesses. The raw scores for two of the vendors, LabStar and Health Systems, have already been entered. Now raw scores must be entered for the third vendor, MedTech. Which vendor's system is best for the Bridgeport Medical Center? Complete these steps to find out:

1. If necessary, start Excel and make sure your Student Disk is in the appropriate disk drive.
2. Open the workbook Medical in the Case folder for Tutorial 1.
3. Use the Save As command to save the workbook as Medical 2 in the Case folder for Tutorial 1. That way you won't change the original workbook for this case.
4. Examine the Evaluation Scores worksheet, and type the following raw scores for MedTech: Cost = 6, Compatibility = 5, Vendor Reliability = 5, Size of Installed Base = 4, User Satisfaction = 5, Critical Functionality = 9, Additional Functionality = 8.
5. Use the Save command to save the modified worksheet.
6. Print the worksheet.
7. Based on the data in the worksheet, which vendor would you recommend? Why?
8. Assume you can adjust the value for only one importance weight (cells B6 through B12). Which factor would you change and what would its new weight be in order for LabStar to have the highest weighted score? (*Hint*: Remember that the value assigned to any importance weight cannot be higher then 10.)
9. Save and print the modified worksheet.

3. Enrollments in the College of Business You work 10 hours a week in the Dean's office at your college. The Assistant Dean has a number of meetings today and has asked you to complete a worksheet she needs for a meeting with Department Chairs this afternoon.

1. Open the workbook Enroll in the Case folder for Tutorial 1 on your Student Disk.
2. Use the Save As command to save the workbook as Enrollment.
3. Complete the workbook by performing the following tasks:
a. Enter the title "Enrollment Data for College of Business" in cell A1.
b. Enter the label "Total" in cell A8.
c. Calculate the total enrollment in the College of Business for 1999 in cell B8.
d. Calculate the total enrollment in the College of Business for 1998 in cell C8.
e. Calculate the change in enrollments from 1998 to 1999. Place the results in column D. Label the column heading "Change" and use the following formula:
Change = 1999 enrollment – 1998 enrollment
4. Save the workbook.
5. Print the worksheet.

4. Krier Marine Services Vince DiOrio is an Information Systems major at a local college. To help pay for tuition, he works part-time three days a week at a nearby marina, Krier Marine Services. Vince works in the business office, and his responsibilities range from making coffee to keeping the company's books.

Recently, Jim Krier, the owner of the marina, asked Vince if he could help computerize the payroll for their part-time employees. He explained that the employees work a different number of hours each week for different rates of pay. Jim does the payroll manually now and finds it time-consuming. Moreover, whenever he makes an error, he is embarrassed and annoyed at having to take the additional time to correct it. Jim was hoping Vince could help him.

Vince immediately agrees to help. He tells Jim that he knows how to use Excel and that he can build a spreadsheet that will save him time and reduce errors. Jim and Vince meet. They review the present payroll process and discuss the desired outcomes of the payroll spreadsheet. Figure 1-30 is a sketch of the output Jim wants to get.

Figure 1-30 ◀
Sketch of worksheet

Krier Marine Services Weekly Payroll
Week Ending 10/15

Employee	Hours	Pay Rate	Gross Pay
Bramble	15	7	formula
Juarez	28	5	"
Smith	30	7	"
DiOrio	22	6	"
Total			formula

1. Open the workbook Payroll in the Cases folder for Tutorial 1 on your Student Disk.
2. Use the Save As command to save the workbook as Payroll 2.
3. Complete the worksheet by performing the following tasks:
   a. Enter the employee hours in column B.
   b. Enter the employee pay rate in column C.
   c. In column D, enter the formulas to compute gross pay for each employee. (*Hint*: Use Hours times Pay Rate.)
   d. In cell D9, enter the SUM function to calculate total gross pay.
4. Save the workbook.
5. Print the worksheet.
6. Remove the hours for the four employees.
7. Enter the following hours: 18 for Bramble, 25 for Juarez, 35 for Smith, and 20 for DiOrio.
8. Print the new worksheet.

Lab Assignments

Spreadsheets

These Lab Assignments are designed to accompany the interactive Course Lab called Spreadsheets. To start the Spreadsheets Lab, click the Start button on the Windows 95 taskbar, point to Programs, point to Course Labs, point to New Perspectives Applications, and click Spreadsheets. If you do not see Course Labs on your Programs menu, see your instructor or technical support person.

Spreadsheets Spreadsheet software is used extensively in business, education, science, and the humanities to simplify tasks that involve calculations. In this Lab you will learn how spreadsheet software works. You will use spreadsheet software to examine and modify worksheets, as well as to create your own worksheets.

1. Click the Steps button to learn how spreadsheet software works. As you proceed through the Steps, answer all of the Quick Check questions that appear. After you complete the Steps, you will see a Quick Check Summary report. Follow the instructions on the screen to print this report.
2. Click the Explore button. Click OK to display a new worksheet. Click File, and then click Open to display the Open dialog box. Click the file Income, then press the Enter key to open the Income and Expense Summary worksheet. Notice that the worksheet contains labels and values for income from consulting and training. It also contains labels and values for expenses such as rent

and salaries. The worksheet does not, however, contain formulas to calculate Total Income, Total Expenses, or Profit. Do the following:

    a. Calculate the Total Income by entering the formula =SUM(C4:C5) in cell C6.

    b. Calculate the Total Expenses by entering the formula =SUM(C9:C12) in cell C13.

    c. Calculate Profit by entering the formula =C6-C13 in cell C15.

    d. Manually check the results to make sure you entered the formulas correctly.

    e. Print your completed worksheet that shows your results.

3. You can use a spreadsheet to keep track of your grade in a class. Click the Explore button to display a blank worksheet. Click File and then click Open to display the Open dialog box. Click the file Grades to open the Grades worksheet. This worksheet contains all the labels and formulas necessary to calculate your grade based on four test scores.

    Suppose you receive a score of 88 out of 100 on the first test. On the second test, you score 42 out of 48. On the third test, you score 92 out of 100. You have not taken the fourth test yet. Enter the appropriate data on the Grade worksheet to determine your grade after taking three tests. Print out your worksheet.

4. Worksheets are handy for answering "what if" questions. For example, suppose you decide to open a lemonade stand. You're interested in how much profit you can make each day. What if you sell 20 cups of lemonade? What if you sell 100? What if the cost of lemons increases?

    In Explore, open the file Lemons and use the worksheet to answer questions a through d, then print the worksheet for item e:

    a. What is your profit if you sell 20 cups a day?

    b. What is your profit if you sell 100 cups a day?

    c. What is your profit if the price of lemons increases to $.07 and you sell 100 cups?

    d. What is your profit if you raise the price of a cup of lemonade to $.30? (Lemons still cost $.07 and you assume you will sell 100 cups.)

    e. Suppose your competitor boasts that she sold 50 cups of lemonade in one day and made exactly $12.00. On your worksheet, adjust the cost of cups, water, lemons, and sugar, and the price per cup to show a profit of exactly $12.00 for 50 cups sold. Print this worksheet.

5. It is important to make sure the formulas in your worksheet are accurate. An easy way to test this is to enter 1s for all the values on your worksheet, and then check the calculations manually. In Explore, open the worksheet Receipt, which calculates sales receipts. Enter 1 as the value for Item 1, Item 2, and Item 3. Enter .01 for the Sales Tax rate. Now, manually calculate what you would pay for three items that cost $1.00 each in a state where sales tax is 1% (.01). Do your manual calculations match those of the worksheet? If not, correct the formulas in the worksheet and print out a formula report of your revised worksheet.

6. In Explore, create your own worksheet showing your household budget for one month. Make sure you put a title on the worksheet. Use formulas to calculate your total income and your total expenses for the month. Add another formula to calculate how much money you were able to save. Print a formula report of your worksheet. Also, print your worksheet, showing realistic values for one month.

Creating a Worksheet

Producing a Sales Comparison Report for MSI

OBJECTIVES

In this tutorial you will:

- Plan, build, test, document, preview, and print a worksheet

- Enter labels, values, and formulas

- Calculate a total using the AutoSum button

- Copy formulas using the fill handle and Clipboard

- Learn about relative, absolute, and mixed references

- Use the AVERAGE, MAX, and MIN functions to calculate values in the worksheet

- Spell check the worksheet

- Insert a row

- Reverse an action using the Undo button

- Move a range of cells

- Format the worksheet using AutoFormat

- Center printouts on a page

- Customize worksheet headers

CASE

Motorcycle Specialties Incorporated

Motorcycle Specialties Incorporated (MSI), a motorcycle helmet and accessories company, provides a wide range of specialty items to motorcycle enthusiasts throughout the world. MSI has its headquarters in Atlanta, Georgia, but it markets its products in North America, South America, Australia, and Europe.

The company's Marketing and Sales Director, Sally Caneval, meets regularly with the regional sales managers who oversee global sales in each of the four regions in which MSI does business. This month, Sally intends to review overall sales in each region for the last two fiscal years and present her findings at her next meeting with the regional sales managers. She has asked you to help her put together a report that summarizes this sales information.

Specifically, Sally wants the report to show total sales for each region of the world for the two most recent fiscal years. Additionally, she wants to see the percentage change between the two years. She also wants the report to include the percentage each region contributed to the total sales of the company in 1999. Finally, she wants to include summary statistics on the average, maximum, and minimum sales for 1999.

SESSION 2.1

In this session you will learn how to plan and build a worksheet; enter labels, numbers, and formulas; and copy formulas to other cells.

Developing Worksheets

Effective worksheets are well planned and carefully designed. A well-designed worksheet should clearly identify its overall goal. It should present information in a clear, well-organized format, and include all the data necessary to produce the results that address the goal of the application.

Further, the process of developing a good worksheet includes the following planning and execution steps:

- Determine the worksheet's purpose, what it will include, and how it will be organized
- Enter the data and formulas into the worksheet
- Test the worksheet
- Edit the worksheet to correct any errors or make modifications
- Document the worksheet
- Improve the appearance of the worksheet
- Save and print the completed worksheet

Planning the Worksheet

Sally begins developing a worksheet that compares global sales by region over two years by first creating a planning analysis sheet. Her **planning analysis sheet** helps her answer the following questions:

1. What is the goal of the worksheet? This helps to define the problem to solve.

2. What are the desired results? This information describes the **output**—the information required to help solve the problem.

3. What data is needed to calculate the results you want to see? This information is the **input**—data that must be entered.

4. What calculations are needed to produce the desired output? These calculations specify the formulas used in the worksheet.

Sally's completed planning analysis sheet is shown in Figure 2-1.

Figure 2-1 ◄
Planning
analysis sheet

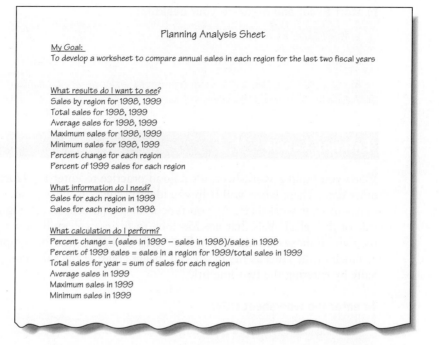

Planning Analysis Sheet

My Goal:
To develop a worksheet to compare annual sales in each region for the last two fiscal years

What results do I want to see?
Sales by region for 1998, 1999
Total sales for 1998, 1999
Average sales for 1998, 1999
Maximum sales for 1998, 1999
Minimum sales for 1998, 1999
Percent change for each region
Percent of 1999 sales for each region

What information do I need?
Sales for each region in 1999
Sales for each region in 1998

What calculation do I perform?
Percent change = (sales in 1999 – sales in 1998)/sales in 1998
Percent of 1999 sales = sales in a region for 1999/total sales in 1999
Total sales for year = sum of sales for each region
Average sales in 1999
Maximum sales in 1999
Minimum sales in 1999

Next, Sally makes a rough sketch of her design, including titles, column headings, row labels, and where data values and totals should be placed. Figure 2-2 shows Sally's sketch. With these two planning tools, Sally is now ready to enter the data into Excel and build the worksheet.

Figure 2-2 ◄
Sketch of
worksheet

Motorcycle Specialties Incorporated
Sales Comparison 1999 with 1998

Region	Year 1999	Year 1998	% Change	% of 1999 Sales
North America	365000	314330	0.16	0.28
South America	354250	292120	0.21	0.28
Australia	251140	262000	-0.04	0.19
Europe	310440	279996	0.11	0.24
Total	1280830	1148446	0.12	

Average	320207.5	
Maximum	365000	
Minimum	251140	

Building the Worksheet

You will use Sally's planning analysis sheet, Figure 2-1, and the rough sketch shown in Figure 2-2 to guide you in preparing the sales comparison worksheet. You will begin by establishing the layout of the worksheet by entering titles and column headings. Next you will work on inputting the data and formulas that will calculate the results Sally needs.

To start Excel and organize your desktop:

1. Start Excel as usual.

2. Make sure your Student Disk is in the appropriate disk drive.

3. Make sure the Microsoft Excel and Book1 windows are maximized.

Entering Labels

When you build a worksheet, it's a good practice to enter the labels before entering any other data. These labels will help you identify the cells where you will enter data and formulas in your worksheet. As you type a label in a cell, Excel aligns the label at the left side of the cell. Labels that are too long to fit in a cell spill over into the cell or cells to the right, if those cells are empty. If the cells to the right are not empty, Excel displays only as much of the label as fits in the cell. Begin creating the sales comparison worksheet for Sally by entering the two-line title.

To enter the worksheet title:

1. If necessary, click cell **A1** to make it the active cell.

2. Type **Motorcycle Specialties Incorporated** and press the **Enter** key. Since cell A1 is empty, the title appears in cell A1 and spills over into cells B1, C1, and D1. Cell A2 is now the active cell.

   TROUBLE? If you make a mistake while typing, remember that you can correct errors with the Backspace key. If you notice the error only after you have pressed the Enter key, then double-click the cell to activate Edit mode, and use the edit keys on your keyboard to correct the error.

3. In cell A2 type **Sales Comparison 1999 with 1998** and press the **Enter** key.

Next, you will enter the column headings defined on the worksheet sketch in Figure 2-2.

To enter labels for the column headings:

1. If necessary, click cell **A3** to make it the active cell.

2. Type **Region** and press the → key to complete the entry. Cell B3 is the active cell.

3. In cell **B3** type **Year 1999** and press the → key.

   Sally's sketch shows that three more column heads are needed for the worksheet. Enter those next.

4. Enter the remaining column heads as follows:
   Cell C3: **Year 1998**
   Cell D3: **% Change**
   Cell E3: **% of 1999 Sales**
   See Figure 2-3.

   TROUBLE? If any cell does not contain the correct label, either edit the cell or retype the entry.

Figure 2-3
Worksheet
after titles and
column
headings
entered

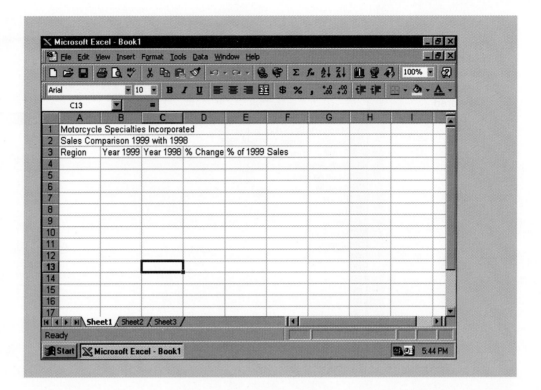

Recall that MSI conducts business in four different regions of the world, and the spreadsheet needs to track the sales information for each region. So Sally wants labels reflecting the regions entered into the worksheet. Enter these labels next.

To enter the regions:

1. Click cell **A4**, type **North America,** and press the **Enter** key.

2. In cell A5 type **South America,** and press the **Enter** key.

3. Type **Australia** in cell A6, and **Europe** in cell A7.

The last set of labels to be entered identify the summary information that will be included in the report.

To enter the summary labels:

1. In cell A8 type **Total** and press the **Enter** key.

2. Type the following labels into the specified cells:
Cell A9: **Average**
Cell A10: **Maximum**
Cell A11: **Minimum**
See Figure 2-4.

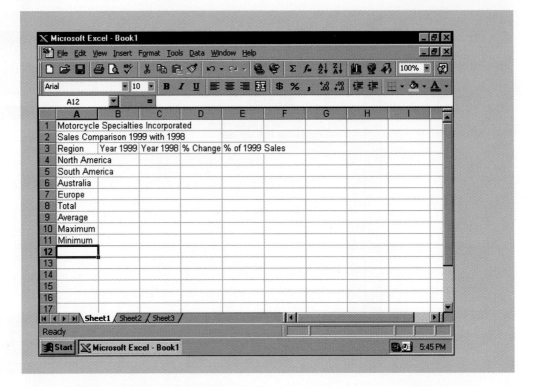

Figure 2-4
Worksheet
after all labels
have been
entered

The labels that you just entered into the worksheet will help to identify where the data and formulas need to be placed.

Entering Data

Recall that values can be numbers, formulas, or functions. The next step in building the worksheet is to enter the data, which in this case is the numbers representing sales in each region during 1998 and 1999.

To enter the sales values for 1998 and 1999:

1. Click cell **B4** to make it the active cell. Type **365000** and press the **Enter** key. See Figure 2-5. Notice that the region name, North America, is no longer completely displayed in cell A4 because cell B4 is no longer empty. Later in the tutorial you will learn how to increase the width of a column in order to display the complete contents of cells.

Figure 2-5 ◀
Worksheet with
label truncated
in cell

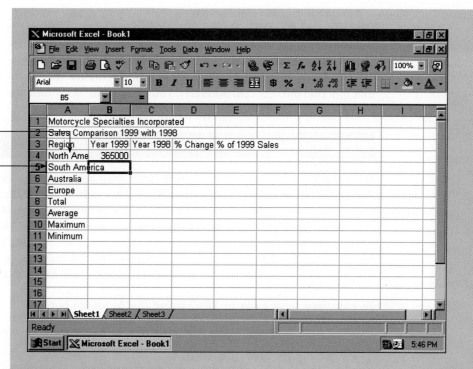

label truncated ——

label spills over
to cell B5

2. In cell B5 type **354250** and press the **Enter** key.

3. Enter the values for cells B6, **251140**, and B7, **310440**.

   Next, type the values for sales during 1998.

4. Click cell **C4**, type **314330**, and press the **Enter** key.

5. Enter the remaining values in the specified cells as follows:
   Cell C5: **292120**
   Cell C6: **262000**
   Cell C7: **279996**
   Your screen should now look like Figure 2-6.

Figure 2-6 ◀
Worksheet
after sales for
1998 and 1999
entered

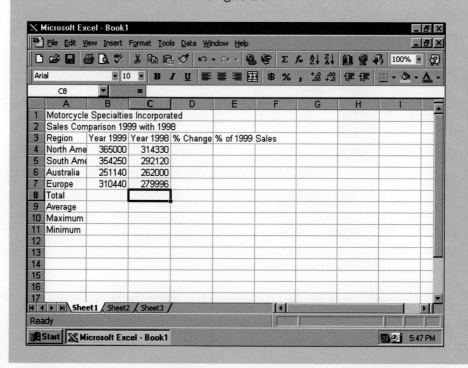

Now that you have entered the labels and data, you need to enter the formulas that will calculate the data to produce the output, or the results. The first calculation Sally wants to see is the total sales for each year. To determine total sales for 1999, you would simply sum the sales from each region for that year. In the previous tutorial you used the SUM function to calculate the weighted total score for the Scottsdale golf site by typing that function into the cell. Similarly, you can use the SUM function to calculate total sales for each year for MSI's comparison report.

Using the AutoSum Button

Since the SUM function is used more often than any other function, Excel includes the AutoSum button on the Standard toolbar. This button automatically creates a formula that contains the SUM function. To do this, Excel looks at the cells adjacent to the active cell, makes an assumption as to which cells you want to sum, and displays a formula based on its best determination about the range you want to sum. You can press the Enter key to accept the formula, or you can select a different range of cells to change the range in the formula. You will use the AutoSum button to calculate the total sales for each year.

To calculate total sales in 1999 using the AutoSum button:

1. Click cell **B8** because this is where you want to display the total sales for 1999.

2. Click the **AutoSum** button 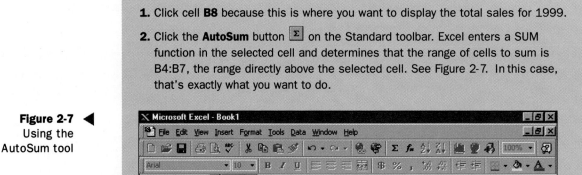 on the Standard toolbar. Excel enters a SUM function in the selected cell and determines that the range of cells to sum is B4:B7, the range directly above the selected cell. See Figure 2-7. In this case, that's exactly what you want to do.

Figure 2-7 ◀
Using the
AutoSum tool

outline of cells
to be summed

range of cells
to be summed

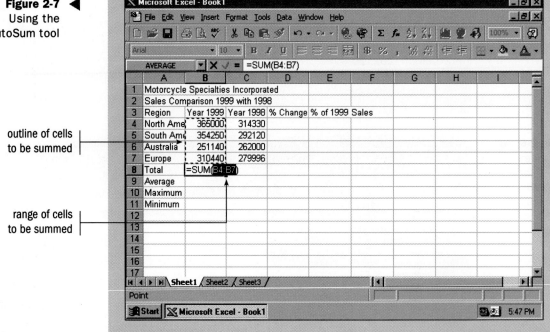

3. Press the **Enter** key to complete the formula. The result, 1280830, appears in cell B8.

Now use the same approach to calculate the total sales for 1998.

Excel

To calculate total sales in 1998 using the AutoSum button:

1. Click cell **C8** to make it the active cell.

2. Click the **AutoSum** button ⟦Σ⟧ on the Standard toolbar.

3. Press the **Enter** key to complete the formula. The result, 1148446, appears in cell C8.

Next, you need to enter the formula to calculate the percent change in sales for North America between 1999 and 1998.

Entering Formulas

Recall that a formula is an equation that performs calculations in a cell. By entering an equal sign (=) as the first entry in the cell, you are telling Excel that the numbers or symbols that follow constitute a formula, not just data. Reviewing Sally's worksheet plan, you note that you need to calculate the percent change in sales in North America. The formula is:

percent change in sales for North America =
(1999 sales in North America - 1998 sales in North America)/1998 sales in North America

So, in looking at the worksheet, the formula in Excel would be:

(B4-C4)/C4

If a formula contains more than one arithmetic operator, Excel performs the calculations in the standard order of precedence of operators shown in Figure 2-8. The **order of precedence** is a set of predefined rules that Excel uses to calculate a formula unambiguously by determining which part of the formula to calculate first, which part second, and so on.

Figure 2-8 ◀
Order of
precedence
operations

Order	Operator	Description
1	^	Exponentiation
2	* or /	Multiplication or division
3	+ or –	Addition or subtraction

Exponentiation has the highest rank, followed by multiplication and division, and finally addition and subtraction. For example, because multiplication has precedence over addition, in the formula =3+4*5 the result of the formula is 23.

When a formula contains more than one operator with the same order of precedence, Excel performs the operation from left to right. Thus, in the formula =4*10/8, Excel multiplies 4 by 10 before dividing the product by 8. The result of the calculation is 5. You can enter parentheses in a formula to make it easier to understand or to change the order of operations. Excel always performs any calculations contained in parentheses first. In the formula =3+4*5, the multiplication is performed before the addition. If instead you wanted the formula to add 3+4 and then multiply the sum by 5, you would enter the formula =(3+4)*5. The result of the calculation is 35.

Now enter the percent change formula as specified in Sally's planning sheet.

To enter the formula for the percent change in sales for North America:

1. Click cell **D4** to make it the active cell.

2. Type **=(B4-C4)/C4** and press the **Enter** key. Excel performs the calculations and displays the value 0.1612 in cell D4. The formula is no longer visible in the cell. If you select the cell, the result of the formula appears in the cell, and the formula you entered appears in the formula bar.

Next, you need to enter the percent change formulas for the other regions, as well as the percent change for the total company sales. You could type the formula =(B5-C5)/C5 in cell D5, the formula =(B6-C6)/C6 in cell D6, the formula =(B7-C7)/C7 in cell D7, and the formula =(B8-C8)/C8 in cell D8. However, this approach is time-consuming and error prone. Instead, you can copy the formula you entered in cell C4 (percent change in North American sales) into cells D5, D6, D7, and D8. **Copying** duplicates the underlying formula in a cell into other cells, automatically adjusting cell references to reflect the new cell address. Copying formulas from one cell to another saves time and reduces the chances of entering incorrect formulas when building worksheets.

Copying a Formula Using the Fill Handle

You can copy formulas using menu commands, toolbar buttons, or the fill handle. The **fill handle** is a small black square located in the lower-right corner of the selected cell, as shown in Figure 2-9. In this section you will use the fill handle to copy the formulas. In other situations you can also use the fill handle for copying values and labels from one cell or a group of cells.

Figure 2-9 ◀
Fill handle

fill handle ———

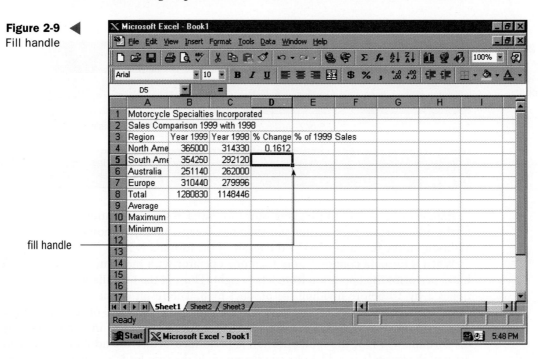

COPYING CELL CONTENTS WITH THE FILL HANDLE

- Click the cell that contains the label, value, or formula you want to copy. If you want to copy the contents of more than one cell, select the range of cells you want to copy.
- To copy to adjacent cells, click and drag the fill handle to outline the cells where you want the copy or copies to appear, and then release the mouse button.

You want to copy the formula from cell D4 to cells D5, D6, D7, and D8.

To copy the formula from cell D4 to cells D5, D6, D7, and D8:

1. Click cell **D4** to make it the active cell.

2. Position the pointer over the fill handle (in the lower-right corner of cell D4) until the pointer changes to $+$.

3. Click and drag the pointer down the worksheet to outline cells D5 through D8. See Figure 2-10.

Figure 2-10 ◄
Copying a
formula

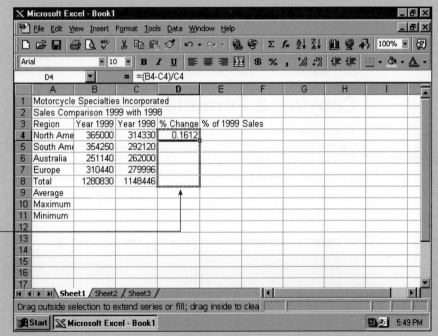

outline of cells
formula will
be copied to

4. Release the mouse button. Excel copies the formula from D4 to cells D5 to D8. Values now appear in cells D5 through D8.

5. Click any cell to deselect the range. See Figure 2-11.

Figure 2-11 ◀
Worksheet
after formula
copied

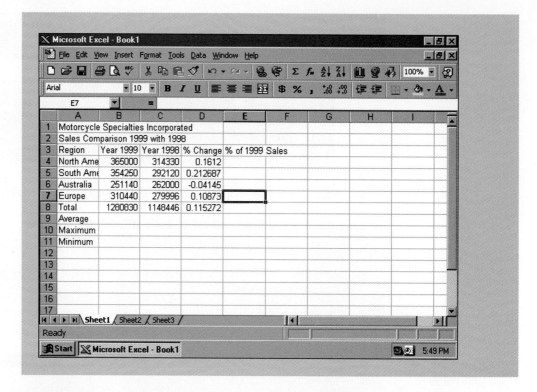

Notice that Excel didn't copy the formula =(B4-C4)/C4 exactly. Rather, it automatically adjusted the cell references for each new formula location. Why did that happen?

Copying a Formula Using Relative References

When you copy a formula that contains cell references, Excel automatically adjusts the cell references for the new locations. For example, when Excel copied the formula from cell D4, =(B4-C4)/C4, it automatically changed the cell references in the formula to reflect the formula's new position in the worksheet. So in cell D5 the cell references adjust to =(B5-C5)/C5. Cell references that change when copied are called **relative cell references**.

Take a moment to look at the formulas in cells D5, D6, D7, and D8.

To examine the formulas in cells D5, D6, D7, and D8:

1. Click cell **D5**. The formula =(B5-C5)/C5 appears in the formula bar.

When Excel copied the formula from cell D4 to cell D5, the cell references changed. The formula =(B4-C4)/C4 became =(B5-C5)/C5 when Excel copied the formula down one row to row 5.

2. Examine the formulas in cells D6, D7, and D8. Notice that the cell references were adjusted for the new locations.

Copying a Formula Using an Absolute Reference

According to Sally's plan, in the worksheet you need to display the percent that each region contributed to the total sales in 1999. For example, if the company's total sales were $100,000 and sales in North America were $25,000, then sales in North America would be 25% of total sales. To complete this calculation for each region you need to divide each region's sales by the total company sales, as shown in the following formulas:

Contribution by North America	=B4/B8
Contribution by South America	=B5/B8
Contribution by Australia	=B6/B8
Contribution by Europe	=B7/B8

First, enter the formula to calculate the percent North America contributed to total sales.

To calculate North America's percent of total 1999 sales:

1. Click cell **E4** to make it the active cell.

2. Type **=B4/B8** and press the **Enter** key to display the value .284971 in cell E4.

Cell E4 displays the correct result. Sales in North America for 1999 were 365,000, which is approximately .28 of the 1,280,830 in total sales in 1999. Next, you decide to copy the formula in cell E4 to cells E5, E6, and E7.

To copy the percent formula in cell E4 to cells E5 through E7:

1. Click cell **E4**, and then move the pointer over the fill handle in cell E4 until it changes to $+$.

2. Click and drag the pointer to cell E7 and release the mouse button.

3. Click any blank cell to deselect the range. The message "#DIV/0!" appears in cells E5 through E7. See Figure 2-12.

Figure 2-12 ◀
Error message
displayed in
worksheet after
copying formula

error message ———

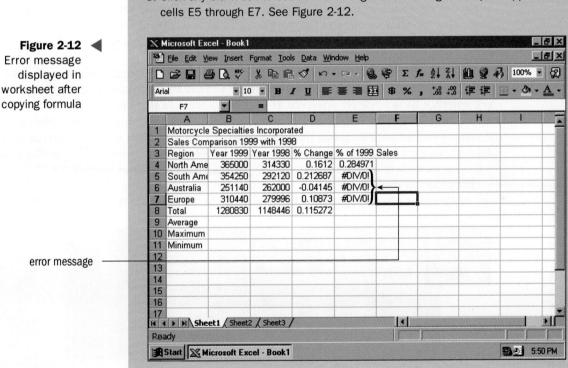

Something is wrong. Cells E5 through E7 display "#DIV/0!," a message that means that Excel was instructed to divide by zero. Take a moment to look at the formulas you copied into cells E5, E6, and E7.

To examine the formulas in cells E5 through E7:

1. Click cell **E5** and look at the formula displayed in the formula bar, =B5/B9. The first cell reference changed from B4 in the original formula to B5 in the copied formula. That's correct because the sales data for South America is entered in cell B5. The second cell reference changed from B8, in the original formula to B9, which is not correct. The correct formula should be =B5/B8 because the total sales are in cell B8, not cell B9.

2. Look at the formulas in cells E6 and E7 and see how the cell references changed in each formula.

As you observed, the cell reference to total company sales (B8) in the original formula was changed to B9, B10, and B11 in the copied formulas. The problem with the copied formulas is that Excel adjusted *all* the cell references relative to their new location.

Absolute Versus Relative References

Sometimes when you copy a formula, you don't want Excel to change all cell references automatically to reflect their new positions in the worksheet. If you want a cell reference to point to the same location in the worksheet when you copy it, you must use an absolute reference. An **absolute reference** is a cell reference in a formula that does not change when copied to another cell.

To create an absolute reference, you insert a dollar sign ($) before the column and row of the cell reference. For example, the cell reference $B$8 is an absolute reference, whereas the cell reference B8 is a relative reference. If you copy a formula that contains the absolute reference $B$8 to another cell, the cell reference to $B$8 does not change. On the other hand, if you copy a formula containing the relative reference B8 to another cell, the reference to B8 changes. In some situations, a cell might have a **mixed reference**, such as $B8; in this case, when the formula is copied, the row number changes but the column letter does not.

To include an absolute reference in a formula, you can type a dollar sign when you type the cell reference, or you can use the F4 key to change the cell reference type while in Edit mode.

REFERENCE window

EDITING CELL REFERENCE TYPES

- Double-click the cell that contains the formula you want to edit.
- Use the arrow keys to move the insertion point to the part of the cell reference you want to change.
- Press the F4 key until the reference is correct.
- Press the Enter key to complete the edit.

To correct the problem in your worksheet, you need to use an absolute reference, instead of a relative reference, to indicate the location of total sales in 1999. That is, you need to change the formula from =B4/B8 to =B4/$B$8. The easiest way to make this change is in Edit mode.

To change a cell reference to an absolute reference:

1. Click cell **E4** to move to the cell that contains the formula you want to edit.

2. Double-click the mouse button to edit the formula in the cell. Notice that each cell reference in the formula in cell E4 appears in a different color and the corresponding cells referred to in the formula are outlined in the same color. This feature is called Range Finder and is designed to make it easier for you to check the accuracy of your formula.

3. Make sure the insertion point is to the right of the division (/) operator, any-where in the cell reference B8.

4. Press the **F4** key to change the reference to $B$8.

   TROUBLE? If your reference shows the **mixed reference** B$8 or $B8, continue to press the F4 key until you see $B$8.

5. Press the **Enter** key to update the formula in cell E4.

Cell E4 still displays .284971, which is the formula's correct result. But remember, the problem in your original formula did not surface until you copied it to cells E5 through E7. To correct the error, you need to copy the revised formula and then check the results. Although you can again use the fill handle to copy the formula, you can also copy the for-mula using the Clipboard and the Copy and Paste buttons on the Standard toolbar.

Copying Cell Contents Using the Copy and Paste Method

You can duplicate the contents of a cell or range by making a copy of the cell or range and then pasting the copy into one or more locations in the same worksheet, another worksheet, or another workbook.

When you copy a cell or range of cells, the copied material is placed on the Clipboard. You can copy labels, numbers, dates, or formulas.

REFERENCE window	**COPYING AND PASTING A CELL OR RANGE OF CELLS**
	■ Select the cell or range of cells to be copied. ■ Click the Copy button on the Standard toolbar. ■ Select the range into which you want to copy the formula. ■ Click the Paste button on the Standard toolbar. ■ Press the Enter key.

You need to copy the formula in cell E4 to the Clipboard and then paste that formula into cells E5 through E7.

To copy the revised formula from cell E4 to cells E5 through E7:

1. Click cell **E4** because it contains the revised formula that you want to copy.

2. Click the **Copy** button on the Standard toolbar. A moving dashed line surrounds cell E4, indicating that the formula has been copied and is available to be pasted into other cells.

3. Click and drag to select cells **E5** through **E7**.

4. Click the **Paste** button on the Standard toolbar. Excel adjusts the formula and pastes it into cells E5 through E7.

5. Click any cell to deselect the range and view the formulas' results. Press the **Escape** key to clear the Clipboard and remove the dashed line surrounding cell E4. See Figure 2-13.

Figure 2-13 ◄
Results of
copying the
formula with
an absolute
reference

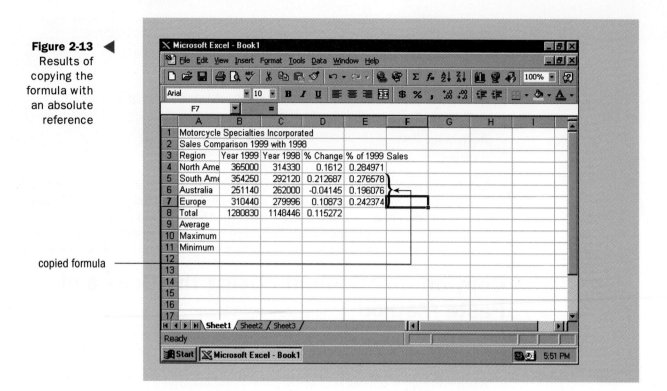

copied formula ─────

Copying this formula worked. When you pasted the formula from cell E4 into the range E5:E7, Excel automatically adjusted the relative reference (B4), while using the cell reference ($B$8) for all absolute references. You have now implemented most of the design as specified in the planning analysis sheet. Now rename the worksheet to accurately describe its contents, then save the workbook to your Student Disk before entering the formulas to compute the summary statistics.

Renaming the Worksheet

Before saving the workbook, look at the sheet tab in the lower-left corner of the worksheet window: the sheet is currently named Sheet1—the name Excel automatically uses when it opens a new workbook. Now that your worksheet is taking shape, you want to give it a more descriptive name that better indicates its contents. Change the worksheet name to Sales Comparison.

To change a worksheet name:

1. Double-click the **Sheet1** sheet tab to select it.

2. Type the new name, **Sales Comparison**, over the current name, Sheet1. Click any cell in the worksheet. The sheet tab displays the name "Sales Comparison."

Saving the New Workbook

Now you want to save the workbook. Because this is the first time you have saved this workbook, you will use the Save As command and name the file MSI Sales Report.

To save the workbook as MSI Sales Report:

1. Click **File** on the menu bar, and then click **Save As** to display the Save As dialog box.

2. In the File name text box, type **MSI Sales Report** but don't press the Enter key yet. You still need to check some other settings.

3. Click the **Save in** list arrow, and then click the drive containing your Student Disk.

4. In the folder list, double-click the **Tutorial.02** folder to select the folder into which you want to save the workbook. Your Save As dialog box should look like the dialog box in Figure 2-14.

Figure 2-14 ◄
Saving the
worksheet as
MSI Sales
Report

enter name of
worksheet here

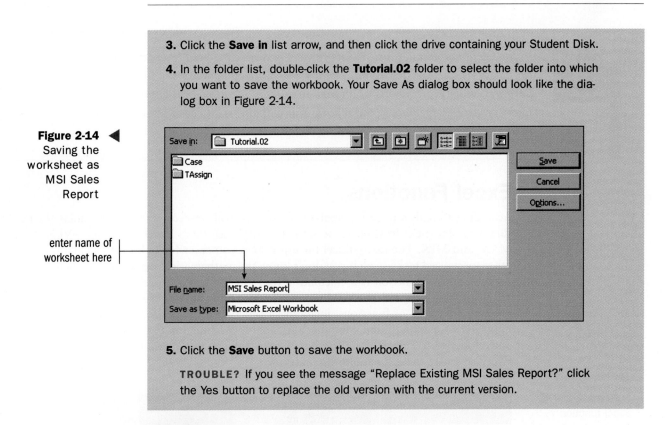

5. Click the **Save** button to save the workbook.

TROUBLE? If you see the message "Replace Existing MSI Sales Report?" click the Yes button to replace the old version with the current version.

Quick Check

1 Describe how AutoSum works.

2 In cell C5 you have the formula =A5+B5. After you copy this formula to cell C6, the formula in cell C6 would appear in the formula bar as _____.

3 In the formula =A5+B5, A5 and B5 are examples of _____ references.

4 In the formula =A8+(1+$C$1), $C$1 is an example of a(n) _____.

5 When you copy a formula using the Copy 🖺 and Paste 🖺 buttons on the Standard toolbar, Excel uses the _____ to temporarily store the formula.

6 The _____ is a small black square located in the lower-right corner of a selected cell.

7 Describe the steps you take to change the name of the sheet tab.

8 List the steps to follow to create a worksheet.

Now that you have planned and built the Sales Comparison worksheet by entering labels, values, and formulas, you need to complete the worksheet by entering some functions and format the worksheet. You will do this in Session 2.2.

SESSION

2.2

In this session you will finish the worksheet as you learn how to enter several statistical functions, increase the column width, insert a row between the titles and column headings, move the contents of a range to another location, and apply one of the Excel predefined formats to the report. You will also spell check the worksheet, and preview and print it.

Excel Functions

According to Sally's planning analysis sheet, you still need to enter the formulas for the summary statistics. To enter these statistics you'll use three Excel functions, AVERAGE, MAX, and MIN. The many Excel functions help you enter formulas for calculations and other specialized tasks, even if you don't know the mathematical details of the calculations. As you recall, a function is a calculation tool that performs a predefined operation. You are already familiar with the SUM function, which adds the values in a range of cells. Excel provides hundreds of functions, including a function to calculate the average of a list of numbers, a function to find a number's square root, a function to calculate loan payments, and a function to calculate the number of days between two dates. Figure 2-15 shows how Excel organizes these functions into categories.

Figure 2-15 ◀
Excel function
categories

Function Category	Examples of Functions in This Category
Financial	Calculate loan payments, depreciation, interest rate, internal rate of return
Date & Time	Display today's date and/or time; calculate the number of days between two dates
Math & Trig	Round off numbers; calculate sums, logs, and least common multiple; generate random numbers
Statistical	Calculate average, standard deviation, and frequencies; find minimum, maximum; count how many numbers are in a list
Lookup & Reference	Look for a value in a range of cells; find the row or column location of a reference
Database	Perform crosstabs, averages, counts, and standard deviation for an Excel database
Text	Convert numbers to text; compare two text entries; find the length of a text entry
Logical	Perform conditional calculations
Information	Return information about the formatting, location, or contents of a range

Each function has a **syntax**, which specifies the order in which you must type the parts of the function and where to put commas, parentheses, and other punctuation. The general syntax of an Excel function is:

$$NAME(\textit{argument1,argument2,...})$$

The syntax of most functions requires you to type the function name followed by one or more arguments in parentheses. Function **arguments** specify the values that Excel must use in the calculation, or the cell references that Excel must include in the calculation. For example, in the function SUM(A1:A20) the function name is SUM and the argument is A1:A20, which is the range of cells you want to total.

Excel

You can use a function in a simple formula such as =SUM(A1:A20), or a more complex formula such as =SUM(A1:A20)*52. As with all formulas, you enter the formula that contains a function in the cell where you want to display the results. The easiest way to enter a function in a cell is to use the Paste Function button on the Standard toolbar, which leads you step-by-step through the process of entering a formula containing a function.

If you prefer, you can type the function directly into the cell. Although the function name is always shown in uppercase, you can type it in either uppercase or lowercase. Also, even though parentheses enclose the arguments, you need not type the closing parenthesis if the function ends the formula. Excel automatically adds the closing parenthesis when you press the Enter key to complete the formula.

According to Sally's planning analysis sheet, the next step is to calculate the average regional sales for 1999.

AVERAGE Function

AVERAGE is a statistical function that calculates the average, or the arithmetic mean. The syntax for the AVERAGE function is:

AVERAGE(*number1,number2,...*)

Generally, when you use the AVERAGE function, *number* is a range of cells. To calculate the average of a range of cells, Excel sums the values in the range, then divides by the number of non-blank cells in the range.

REFERENCE window

USING THE PASTE FUNCTION BUTTON

- Click the cell where you want to display the results of the function. Then click the Paste Function button on the Standard toolbar to open the Paste Function dialog box.
- Click the type of function you want in the Function category list box.
- Click the function you want in the Function name list box.
- Click the OK button to open a second dialog box.
- Accept the default information or enter the information you want the function to use in its calculations.
- Click the OK button to close the dialog box and display the results of the function in the cell.

Sally wants you to calculate the average sales in 1999. You'll use the Paste Function button to enter the AVERAGE function, which is one of the statistical functions.

To enter the AVERAGE function using the Paste Function button:

1. Click cell **B9** to select the cell where you want to enter the AVERAGE function.

2. Click the **Paste Function** button on the Standard toolbar to display the Paste Function dialog box.

   TROUBLE? If the Office Assistant opens and offers help on this feature, click the No option button.

3. Click **Statistical** in the Function category list box.

4. Click **AVERAGE** in the Function name list box. See Figure 2-16. The syntax for the AVERAGE function, AVERAGE(*number1,number2,...*), is displayed beneath the Function category box.

Figure 2-16 ◀
Paste Function
dialog box

syntax for
AVERAGE Function

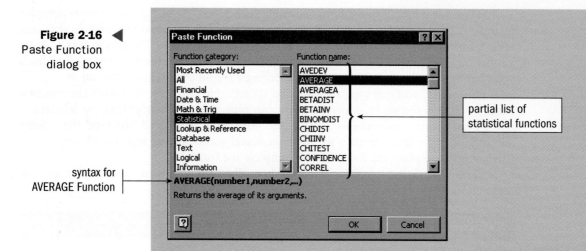

partial list of
statistical functions

5. Click the **OK** button to open the AVERAGE dialog box. Notice that the range B4:B8 appears in the Number1 text box, and =AVERAGE(B4:B8) appears in the formula bar. See Figure 2-17.

Figure 2-17 ◀
AVERAGE
dialog box

range includes
cell B8

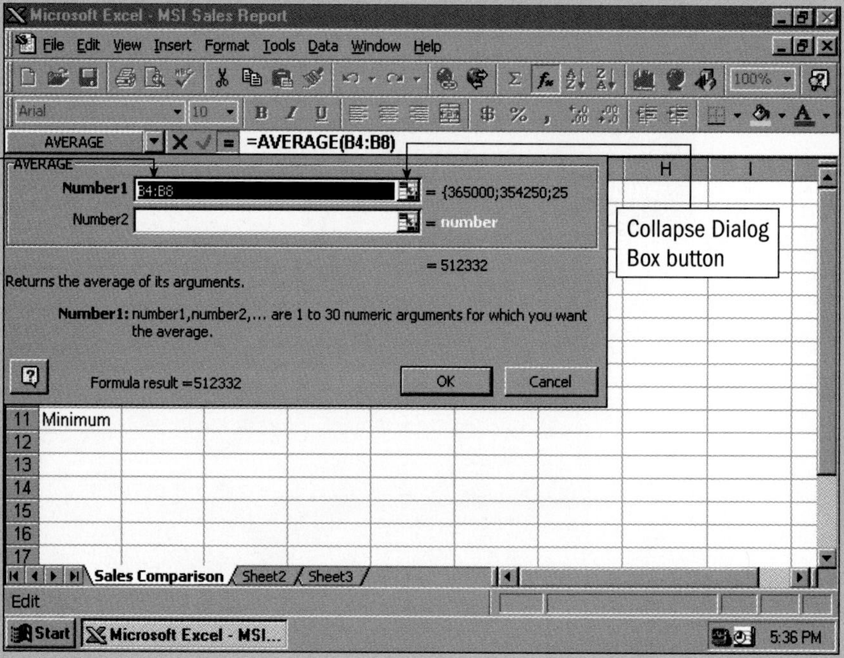

Collapse Dialog
Box button

Excel has incorrectly included the total sales for 1999 (cell B8) in the range to calculate the average. The correct range is B4:B7.

6. Click the **Collapse Dialog Box** button to the right of the Number1 text box to collapse the dialog box to the size of one row. This makes it easier for you to identify and select the correct range.

7. Position the cell pointer over cell **B4**, click and drag to select the range **B4:B7**, and then click the **Collapse Dialog Box** button. The collapsed dialog box is restored and the correct range, B4:B7, is displayed in the Number1 text box. The formula =AVERAGE(B4:B7) is displayed in the formula bar.

8. Click the **OK** button to close the dialog box and return to the worksheet. The average, 320207.5, now appears in cell B9.

According to your plan, you need to enter a formula to find the largest regional sales amount in 1999. To do this, you'll use the MAX function.

MAX Function

MAX is a statistical function that finds the largest number. The syntax of the MAX function is:

$$MAX(number1,number2,...)$$

In the MAX function, *number* can be a constant number such as 345, a cell reference such as B6, or a range of cells such as B5:B16. You can use the MAX function to simply display the largest number or to use the largest number in a calculation. Although you can use the Paste Function to enter the MAX function, this time you'll type the MAX function directly into cell B10.

To enter the MAX function by typing directly into a cell:

1. If necessary, click cell **B10** to select it as the cell into which you want to type the formula that uses the MAX function.

2. Type **=MAX(B4:B7)** and press the **Enter** key. Cell B10 displays 365000, the largest regional sales amount in 1999.

Next, you need to find the smallest regional sales amount in 1999. For that, you'll use the MIN function.

MIN Function

MIN is a statistical function that finds the smallest number. The syntax of the MIN function is:

$$MIN(number1,number2,...)$$

You can use the MIN function to display the smallest number or to use the smallest number in a calculation.

You'll enter the MIN function directly into cell B11, using the pointing method.

Building Formulas by Pointing

Excel provides several ways to enter cell references into a formula. One is to type the cell references directly, as you have done so far in all the formulas you've entered. Another way to put a cell reference in a formula is to **point** to the cell reference you want to include while creating the formula. To use the pointing method to enter the formula, you click the cell or range of cells whose cell references you want to include in the formula. You may prefer to use this method to enter formulas, because it minimizes typing errors.

Now enter the formula to calculate the minimum sales by using the pointing method.

To enter the MIN function using the pointing method:

1. If necessary, click cell **B11** to move to the cell where you want to enter the formula that uses the MIN function.

2. Type **=MIN(** to begin the formula.

3. Position the cell pointer in cell **B4**, and then click and drag to select cells **B4** through **B7**. As you drag the mouse over the range, notice that the message "4Rx1C" appears in a ScreenTip, informing you that four rows and one column have been selected. Release the mouse button, and then press the **Enter** key. Cell B11 displays 251140, the smallest regional sales amount for 1999. See Figure 2-18.

Figure 2-18 ◀
Worksheet
after labels,
numbers,
formulas, and
functions
entered

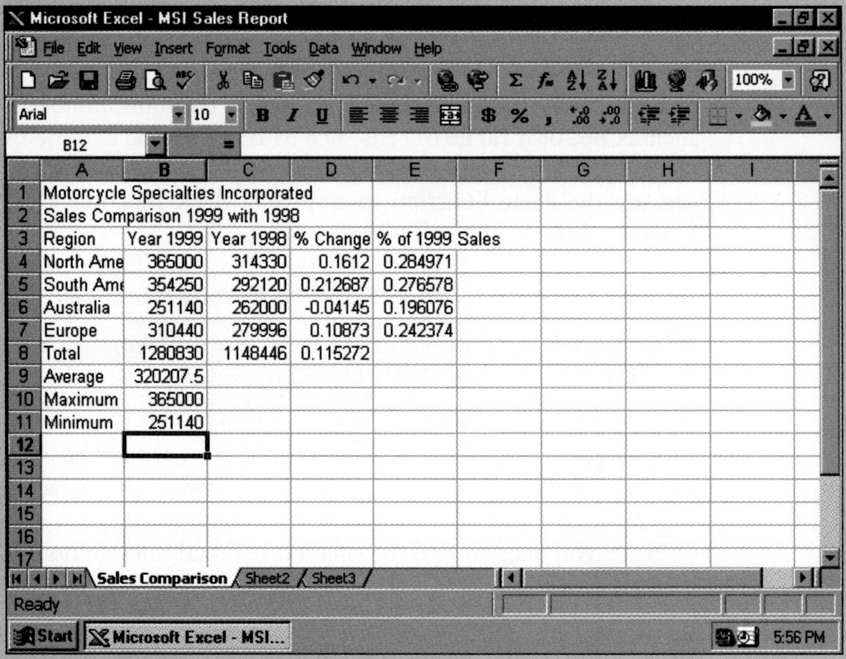

Now that the worksheet labels, values, formulas, and functions have been entered, Sally reviews the worksheet.

Testing the Worksheet

Before trusting a worksheet and its results, you should test it to make sure you entered the correct formulas. You want the worksheet to produce accurate results.

Beginners often expect their Excel worksheets to work correctly the first time. Sometimes they do work correctly the first time, but even well-planned and well-designed worksheets can contain errors. It's best to assume that a worksheet has errors and test it to make sure it is correct. While there are no rules for testing a worksheet, here are some approaches:

■ Entering **test values**, numbers that generate a known result, to determine whether your worksheet formulas are accurate. For example, try entering a 1 into each cell. After you enter the test values, you compare the results in your worksheet with the known results. If the results on your worksheet don't match the known results, you probably made an error.

■ Entering **extreme values**, such as very large or very small numbers, and observing their effect on cells with formulas.

■ Working out the numbers ahead of time with pencil, paper, and calculator, and comparing these results with the output from the computer.

Sally used the third approach to test her worksheet. She had calculated her results using a calculator (Figure 2-2) and then compared them with the results on the screen (Figure 2-18). The numbers agree, so she feels confident that the worksheet she created contains accurate results.

Spell Checking the Worksheet

You can use the Excel spell check feature to help identify and correct spelling and typing errors. Excel compares the words in your worksheet to the words in its dictionary. If Excel finds a word in your worksheet not in its dictionary, it shows you the word and some suggested corrections, and you decide whether to correct it or leave it as is.

REFERENCE window

CHECKING THE SPELLING IN A WORKSHEET

- Click cell A1 to begin the spell check from the top of the worksheet.
- Click the Spelling button on the Standard toolbar.
- Change the spelling or ignore the spell check's suggestion for each identified word.
- Click the OK button when the spell check is complete.

You have tested your numbers and formulas for accuracy. Now you can check the spelling of all text entries in the worksheet.

To check the spelling in a worksheet:

1. Click cell **A1** to begin spell checking in the first cell of the worksheet.

2. Click the **Spelling** button ![spelling icon] on the Standard toolbar to check the spelling of the text in the worksheet. A message box indicates that Excel has finished spell checking the entire worksheet. No errors were found.

   TROUBLE? If the spell check does find a spelling error in your worksheet, use the Spelling dialog box options to correct the spelling mistake and continue checking the worksheet.

Improving the Worksheet Layout

Although the numbers are correct, Sally does not want to present a worksheet without a more polished appearance. She feels that there are a number of simple changes you can make to the worksheet that will improve its layout and make the data more readable. Specifically, she asks you to increase the width of column A so that the entire region names are displayed, insert a blank row between the titles and column headings, move the summary statistics down three rows from their current location, and apply one of the pre-defined Excel formats to the worksheet.

Changing Column Width

Changing the column width is one way to improve the appearance of the worksheet, making it easier to read and interpret data. In Sally's worksheet, you need to increase the width of column A so that the entire labels for North America and South America appear in their cells.

Excel provides several methods for changing column width. For example, you can click a column heading or click and drag the pointer to select a series of column headings and then use the Format menu. You can also use the dividing line between column headings in the column header row. When you move the pointer over the dividing line between two column headings, the pointer changes to ✛. You can then use the pointer to drag the dividing line to a new location. You can also double-click the dividing line to make the column as wide as the longest text label or number in the column.

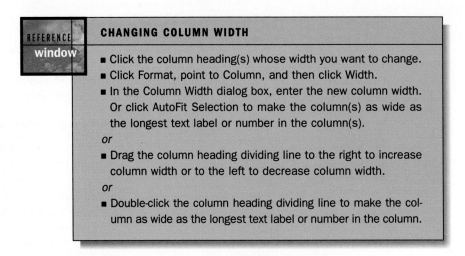

REFERENCE window

CHANGING COLUMN WIDTH

- Click the column heading(s) whose width you want to change.
- Click Format, point to Column, and then click Width.
- In the Column Width dialog box, enter the new column width. Or click AutoFit Selection to make the column(s) as wide as the longest text label or number in the column(s).

or

- Drag the column heading dividing line to the right to increase column width or to the left to decrease column width.

or

- Double-click the column heading dividing line to make the column as wide as the longest text label or number in the column.

Sally has asked you to change column A's width so that the complete region name is displayed.

To change the width of column A:

1. Position the pointer ✛ on the A in the column heading area.

2. Move the pointer to the right edge of the column heading dividing columns A and B. Notice that the pointer changes to the resize arrow ✛.

3. Click and drag the resize arrow to the right, increasing the column width 12 characters or more, as indicated in the ScreenTip that pops up on the screen.

4. Release the mouse button. See Figure 2-19.

Figure 2-19 ◀
Worksheet
after width of
column A
increased

now entire contents
of cell displayed

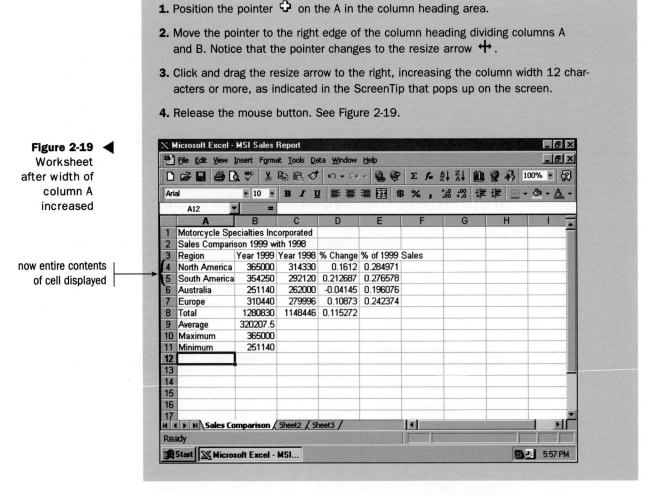

Next, you need to insert a row between the title and the column heading.

Inserting a Row into a Worksheet

At times, you may need to add one or more rows or columns to a worksheet to make room for new data or to make the worksheet easier to read. The process of inserting columns and rows is similar; you select the number of columns or rows you want to insert and then use the Insert command to insert the columns or rows. When you insert rows or columns, Excel repositions other rows and columns in the worksheet and automatically adjusts cell references in formulas to reflect the new location of values used in calculations.

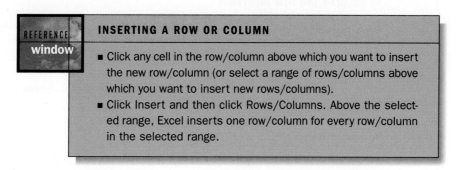

REFERENCE window

INSERTING A ROW OR COLUMN

- Click any cell in the row/column above which you want to insert the new row/column (or select a range of rows/columns above which you want to insert new rows/columns).
- Click Insert and then click Rows/Columns. Above the selected range, Excel inserts one row/column for every row/column in the selected range.

Sally wants one blank row between the titles and column headings in her worksheet.

To insert a row into a worksheet:

1. Click cell **A2**.

2. Click **Insert** on the menu bar, and then click **Rows**. Excel inserts a blank row above the original row 2. All other rows shift down one row. See Figure 2-20.

Figure 2-20 ◀
Worksheet after one row inserted above original row 2

row inserted in wrong position

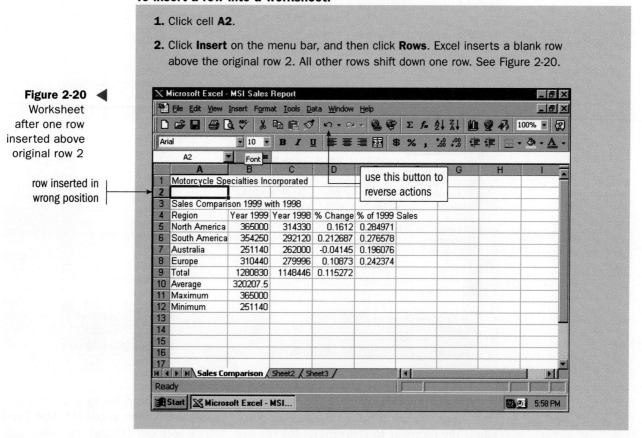

The blank row isn't really where you wanted it. You inserted a row between the two lines of the title instead of between the title and the column heading. To correct this error you can either delete the row or use the Undo button. If you need to delete a row or column, select the row(s) or column(s) you want to delete, then click Delete on the Edit menu, or press the Delete key on your keyboard. You use the Undo button because it is a feature you find valuable in many situations.

Using the Undo Button

The Excel Undo button lets you cancel recent actions one at a time. Click the Undo button to reverse the last command or delete the last entry you typed. To reverse more than one action, click the arrow next to the Undo button and click the action you want to undo on the drop-down list.

Now use the Undo button to reverse the row insertion.

To reverse the row insertion:

1. Click the **Undo** button 🔄 on the Standard toolbar to restore the worksheet to its status before the row was inserted.

Now you can insert the blank row in the correct place—between the second line of the worksheet title and the column heads.

To insert a row into a worksheet:

1. Click cell **A3** because you want to insert one row above row 3. If you wanted to insert several rows, you would select as many rows as you wanted to insert before using the Insert command.

2. Click **Insert** on the menu bar, and then click **Rows**. Excel inserts a blank row above the original row 3. All other rows shift down one row. See Figure 2-21.

Figure 2-21 ◀
Worksheet
after one row
inserted

row inserted in
desired location

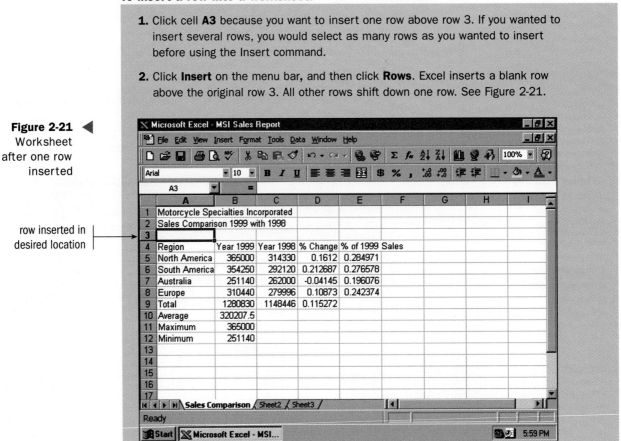

Adding a row changed the location of the data in the worksheet. For example, the percent change in North American sales, originally in cell D4, is now in cell D5. Did Excel adjust the formulas to compensate for the new row? Check cell D5 and any other cells you want to view to verify that the cell references were adjusted.

To examine the formula in cell D5 and other cells:

1. Click cell **D5**. The formula =(B5-C5)/C5 appears in the formula bar. You originally entered the formula =(B4-C4)/C4 in cell D4 to calculate percent change in North America. Excel automatically adjusted the cell reference to reflect the new location of the data.

2. Inspect other cells below row 3 to verify that their cell references were automatically adjusted when the new row was inserted.

Sally has also suggested moving the summary statistics down three rows from the present location to make the report easier to read. So, you will need to move the range of cells containing the average, minimum, and maximum sales to a different location in the worksheet.

Moving a Range Using the Mouse

To place the summary statistics three rows below the other data in the report, you could use the Insert command to insert three blank rows between the total and average sales. Alternatively, you could use the mouse to move the summary statistics to a new location. Since you already know how to insert a row, try using the mouse to move the summary statistics to a new location. This technique is called **drag-and-drop**. You simply select the cell range you want to move and use the pointer to drag the cells' contents to the desired location.

REFERENCE window	**MOVING A RANGE USING THE MOUSE**
	■ Select the cell or range of cells you want to move.
	■ Place the mouse pointer over any edge of the selected range until the pointer changes to an arrow.
	■ Click and drag the outline of the range to the new worksheet location.
	■ Release the mouse button.

Sally has asked you to move the range A10 through B12 to the new destination area A13 through B15.

To move a range of cells using the drag-and-drop technique:

1. Select the range of cells **A10:B12**, which contains the sales summary statistics you want to move.

2. Place the mouse pointer over any edge of the selected range until the pointer changes to an arrow ⬈ . See Figure 2-22.

Figure 2-22 ◄
Range to
be moved

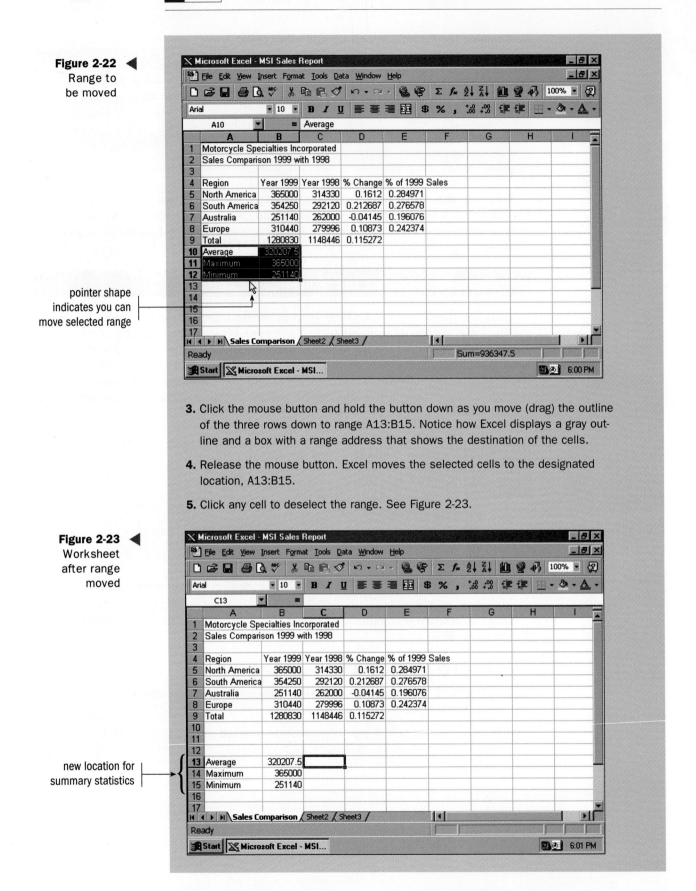

pointer shape
indicates you can
move selected range

3. Click the mouse button and hold the button down as you move (drag) the outline of the three rows down to range A13:B15. Notice how Excel displays a gray outline and a box with a range address that shows the destination of the cells.

4. Release the mouse button. Excel moves the selected cells to the designated location, A13:B15.

5. Click any cell to deselect the range. See Figure 2-23.

Figure 2-23 ◄
Worksheet
after range
moved

new location for
summary statistics

Next, Sally wants you to use the Excel AutoFormat feature to improve the worksheet's appearance by emphasizing the titles and aligning numbers in cells.

Using AutoFormat

The **AutoFormat** feature lets you change your worksheet's appearance by selecting from a collection of predesigned worksheet formats. Each worksheet format in the AutoFormat collection gives your worksheet a more professional appearance by applying attractive fonts, borders, colors, and shading to a range of data. AutoFormat also adjusts column widths, row heights, and the alignment of text in cells to improve the worksheet's appearance.

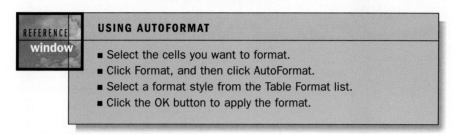

REFERENCE window

USING AUTOFORMAT

- Select the cells you want to format.
- Click Format, and then click AutoFormat.
- Select a format style from the Table Format list.
- Click the OK button to apply the format.

Now you'll use AutoFormat's Simple format to improve the worksheet's appearance.

To apply AutoFormat's Simple format:

1. Select cells **A1:E9** as the range you want to format using AutoFormat.

2. Click **Format** on the menu bar, and then click **AutoFormat**. The AutoFormat dialog box opens. See Figure 2-24.

Figure 2-24 ◀
AutoFormat
dialog box

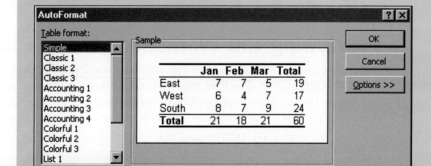

3. The Table format box lists the available formats. The format called "Simple" is selected and the Sample box shows how the Simple format looks when applied to a worksheet.

4. Click each of the formats from Simple down to Accounting 1. Notice the different font styles and colors of each format shown in the Sample box.

5. Click the **Simple** format, and then click the **OK** button to apply this format.

6. Click any cell to deselect the range. Figure 2-25 shows the newly formatted worksheet.

Figure 2-25 ◀
Worksheet
after using the
Simple
AutoFormat

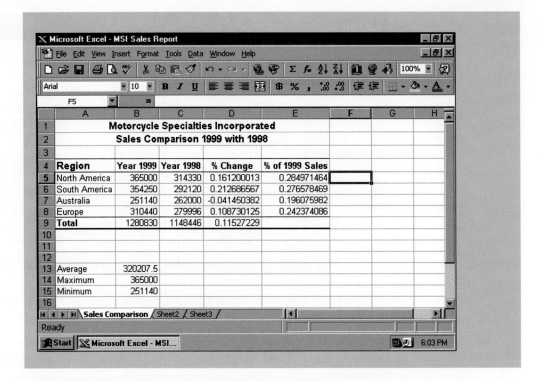

You show the worksheet to Sally. She's impressed with the improved appearance and decides to hand it out to the regional sales managers at their next meeting. She asks you to print it so she can make copies.

Previewing the Worksheet Using Print Preview

Before you print a worksheet, you can use the Excel Print Preview window to see how it will look when printed. The **Print Preview window** shows you margins, page breaks, headers, and footers that are not always visible on the screen. If the preview isn't what you want, you can close the Print Preview window and change the worksheet before printing it.

To preview the worksheet before you print it:

1. Click the **Print Preview** button on the Standard toolbar. After a moment Excel displays the worksheet in the Print Preview window. See Figure 2-26.

Figure 2-26 ◀
Print preview of
sales
comparison
worksheet

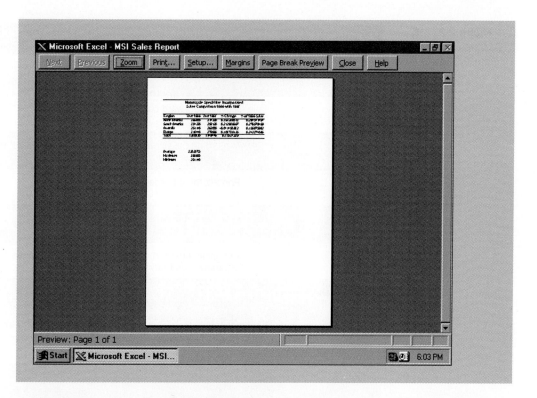

When Excel displays a full page in the Print Preview window, you might have difficulty seeing the text of the worksheet because it is so small. Don't worry if the preview isn't completely readable. One purpose of the Print Preview window is to see the overall layout of the worksheet and how it will fit on the printed page. If you want a better view of the text, you can use the Zoom button.

To display an enlarged section of the Print Preview window:

1. Click the **Zoom** button to display an enlarged section of the Print Preview.

2. Click the **Zoom** button again to return to the full-page view.

Notice that the Print Preview window contains several other buttons. Figure 2-27 describes each of these buttons.

Figure 2-27 ◀
Description of
Print Preview
buttons

Clicking this Button	Results in
Next	Moving forward one page
Previous	Moving backward one page
Zoom	Magnifying the Print Preview screen to zoom in on any portion of the page; click again to return to full-page preview
Print	Printing the document
Setup	Displaying the Page Setup dialog box
Margins	Changing the width of margins, columns in the worksheet and the position of headers and footers
Page Break Preview	Showing where page breaks occur in the worksheet and which area of the worksheet will be printed; you can adjust where data will print by inserting or moving page breaks
Close	Closing the Print Preview window
Help	Activating Help

Looking at the worksheet in Print Preview, you observe that it is not centered on the page. By default, Excel prints a worksheet at the upper left of the page's print area. You can specify that the worksheet be centered vertically, horizontally, or both.

Centering the Printout

Worksheet printouts generally look more professional centered on the printed page. You decide that Sally would want you to center the sales comparison worksheet both horizontally and vertically on the printed page.

To center the printout:

1. Click the **Setup** button to display the Page Setup dialog box.

2. Click the **Margins** tab. See Figure 2-28. Notice that the preview box displays a worksheet positioned at the upper-left edge of the page.

Excel

Figure 2-28 ◀
Margins tab of
Page Setup
dialog box

indicates that
worksheet will be
displayed in upper-
left corner of page

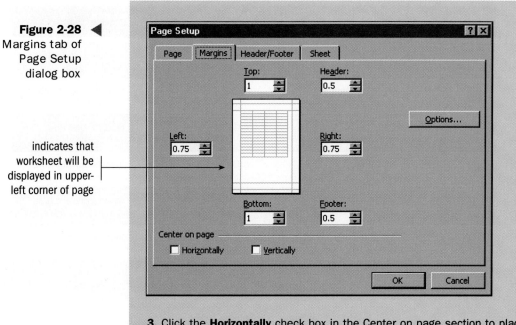

3. Click the **Horizontally** check box in the Center on page section to place a check in it.

4. Click the **Vertically** check box to place a check in it.

   Notice that the sample window shows that the worksheet is now centered vertically and horizontally on the page.

5. Click the **OK** button to return to the Print Preview window. Notice that the output in the Print Preview window is displayed centered vertically and horizontally.

   TROUBLE? If you see only the worksheet name, click the Zoom button to view the entire page.

Adding Headers and Footers

Headers and footers can provide you with useful documentation on your printed worksheet, such as the name of the person who created the worksheet, the date it was printed, and its filename. The **header** is text printed in the top margin of every worksheet page. A **footer** is text printed in the bottom margin of every page. Headers and footers are not displayed in the worksheet window. To see them, you must preview or print the worksheet.

Excel uses formatting codes in headers and footers to represent the items you want to print. Formatting codes produce dates, times, and filenames that you might want a header or footer to include. You can type these codes, or you can click a formatting code button to insert the code. Figure 2-29 shows the formatting codes and the buttons for inserting them.

Figure 2-29 ◀
Header
and footer
formatting
buttons

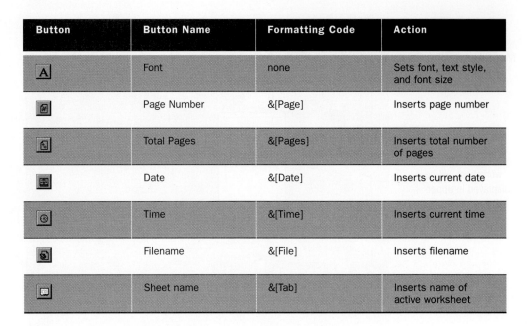

Button	Button Name	Formatting Code	Action
A	Font	none	Sets font, text style, and font size
	Page Number	&[Page]	Inserts page number
	Total Pages	&[Pages]	Inserts total number of pages
	Date	&[Date]	Inserts current date
	Time	&[Time]	Inserts current time
	Filename	&[File]	Inserts filename
	Sheet name	&[Tab]	Inserts name of active worksheet

Sally asks you to add a header that includes the filename and today's date. She also wants you to add a footer that displays the page number.

To add a header and a footer to your worksheet:

1. In the Print Preview window, click the **Setup** button to open the Page Setup dialog box, and then click the **Header/Footer** tab.

2. Click the **Custom Header** button to display the Header dialog box.

3. With the insertion point in the Left section box, click the **Filename** button 🔲. The code &[File] appears in the Left section box.

   TROUBLE? If you clicked the wrong code, double-click the code, press the Delete key, then repeat Steps 2 and 3.

4. Click the **Right section** box to move the insertion point to the Right section box.

5. Click the **Date** button 🔲. The code &[Date] appears in the Right section box. See Figure 2-30.

Figure 2-30 ◀
Inserting
formatting
codes into
the Header
dialog box

formatting code to
display workbook
filename

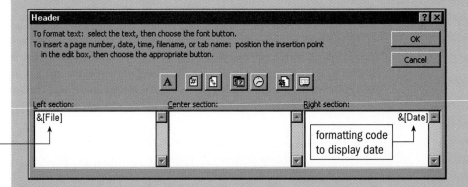

   TROUBLE? If you clicked the wrong code, double-click the code, press the Delete key, then repeat Step 5.

6. Click the **OK** button to complete the header and return to the Page Setup dialog box. Notice that the header shows the filename on the left and the date on the right.

7. Click the **Custom Footer** button to display the Footer dialog box.

8. Click the **Center section** box to move the insertion point to the Center Section box.

9. Click the **Page Number** button 📄. The code &[Page] appears in the Center section box.

10. Click the **OK** button to complete the footer and return to the Page Setup dialog box. Notice that the footer shows the page number in the bottom center of the page.

11. Click the **OK** button to return to the Print Preview window. The changed header appears in the Print Preview window.

12. Click the **Close** button to exit the Print Preview window and return to the worksheet.

You'll use the Print button on the Standard toolbar to print one copy of the worksheet with the current settings. First, save the worksheet before printing it.

To save your page setup settings:

1. Click the **Save** button 💾 on the Standard toolbar.

2. Click the **Print** button 🖨 on the Standard toolbar. See Figure 2-31.

 TROUBLE? If you see a message that indicates that you have a printer problem, click the Cancel button to cancel printing. Check your printer to make sure it is turned on and is online; also make sure it has paper. Then go back and try Step 2 again. If you have no printer available, click the Cancel button.

Figure 2-31 ◀
Printed
worksheet

Motorcycle Specialties Incorporated Sales Comparison 1999 with 1998				
Region	**Year 1999**	**Year 1998**	**% Change**	**% of 1999 Sales**
North America	365000	314330	0.161200013	0.284971464
South America	354250	292120	0.212686567	0.276578469
Australia	251140	262000	-0.041450382	0.196075982
Europe	310440	279996	0.108730125	0.242374086
Total	1280830	1148446	0.11527229	
Average	320207.5			
Maximum	365000			
Minimum	251140			

Sally reviews the printed worksheet and is satisfied with its appearance. She will make four copies to be distributed to the regional managers at the next meeting.

Documenting the Workbook

Documenting the workbook provides valuable information to those using the workbook. Documentation includes external documentation as well as notes and instructions within the workbook. This information could be as basic as who created the worksheet and the date it was created, or it could be more detailed, summarizing formulas and layout.

Depending on the use of the workbook, the required amount of documentation varies. Sally's planning analysis sheet and sketch for the sales comparison worksheet are one form of external documentation. This information can be useful to someone who would need to modify the worksheet in any way because it states the goals, required input, output, and the calculations used.

One source of internal documentation would be a worksheet that is placed as the first worksheet in the workbook, such as the Title Sheet worksheet in the workbook you worked with in Tutorial 1 to determine the best location for the new Inwood golf course. In more complex workbooks, this sheet may also include an index of all worksheets in the workbook, instructions on how to use the worksheets, where to enter data, how to save the workbook, and how to print reports. This documentation method is useful because the information is contained directly in the workbook and can easily be viewed upon opening the workbook, or printed if necessary. Another source of internal documentation is the **Property dialog box**. This dialog box enables you to electronically capture information such as the name of the workbook's creator, the creation date, the number of revisions, and other information related to the workbook.

If you prefer, you can include documentation in each sheet of the workbook. One way is to attach notes to cells by using the Comments command to explain complex formulas and assumptions.

The worksheet itself can be used as documentation. Once a worksheet is completed, it is a good practice to print and file a "hard" copy of your work as documentation. This hard copy file should include a printout of each worksheet with the values displayed and another printout of the worksheet displaying the cell formulas.

Displaying and Printing Worksheet Formulas

You can document the formulas you entered in a worksheet by displaying and printing them. When you display formulas, Excel shows the formulas you entered in each cell instead of showing the results of the calculations. You want a printout of the formulas in your worksheet for documentation.

To display worksheet formulas:

1. Click **Tools** on the menu bar, and then click **Options** to open the Options dialog box.

2. Click the **View** tab, and then click the **Formulas** check box in the Window options section to place a check in it.

3. Click the **OK** button to return to the worksheet. The width of each column nearly doubles to accommodate the underlying formulas. See Figure 2-32.

Figure 2-32 ◀
Displaying
formulas in a
worksheet

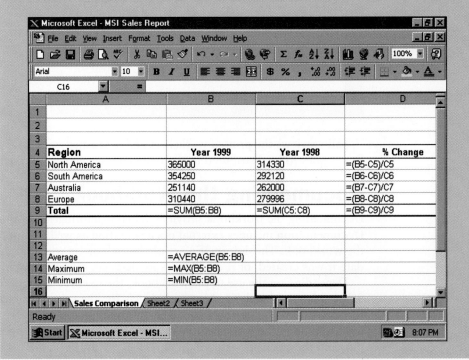

Now print the worksheet with the formulas displayed. Before printing the formulas you need to change the appropriate settings in the Page Setup dialog box to show the gridlines and the row/column headings, center the worksheet on the page, and fit the printout on a single page.

To adjust the print setups to display formulas:

1. Click **File** on the menu bar, and then click **Page Setup** to display the Page Setup dialog box.

2. Click the **Sheet** tab to view the sheet options. Click the **Row and Column Headings** check box to print the row numbers and column letters along with the worksheet results.

3. Click the **Gridlines** check box to place a check in it and select that option.

4. Click the **Page** tab, and then click the **Landscape** option button. This option prints the worksheet with the paper position so it is wider than it is tall.

5. Click the **Fit to** option button in the Scaling section of the Page tab. This option reduces the worksheet when you print it, so it fits on the specific number of pages in the Fit to check box. The default is 1.

6. Click the **Print Preview** button to open the Print Preview window.

7. Click the **Print** button. See Figure 2-33.

Figure 2-33 ◀
Printout of
worksheet
formulas

	A	B	C	D	E
1					
2					
3					
4	Region	Year 1999	Year 1998	% Change	% of 1999 Sales
5	North America	365000	314330	=(B5-C5)/C5	=B5/$B$9
6	South America	354250	292120	=(B6-C6)/C6	=B6/$B$9
7	Australia	251140	262000	=(B7-C7)/C7	=B7/$B$9
8	Europe	310440	279996	=(B8-C8)/C8	=B8/$B$9
9	Total	=SUM(B5:B8)	=SUM(C5:C8)	=(B9-C9)/C9	
10					
11					
12					
13	Average	=AVERAGE(B5:B8)			
14	Maximum	=MAX(B5:B8)			
15	Minimum	=MIN(B5:B8)			

After printing the formulas, return the worksheet so it displays the worksheet values.

To turn off the formulas display:

1. Click **Tools** on the menu bar, and then click **Options** to open the Options dialog box.

2. Click the **View** tab if necessary, and then click **Formulas** to remove the check mark next to that option to deselect it.

3. Click the **OK** button to return to the worksheet. The formulas are no longer displayed.

4. Close the workbook and exit Excel.

Quick Check

1 To move a range of cells, you must _____ the range first.

2 A _____ is text that is printed in the top margin of every worksheet page.

3 _____ is a command that lets you change your worksheet's appearance by selecting a collection of predesigned worksheet formats.

4 Describe how to insert a row or a column.

5 To reverse your most recent action, which button should you click?
   a. 🖫
   b. 📂
   c. ↺

6 Describe how you use the pointing method to create a formula.

7 To display formulas instead of values in your worksheet, you choose what command?

8 If your worksheet has too many columns to fit on one printed page, you should try _____ orientation.

You have planned, built, formatted, and documented Sally's sales comparison worksheet. It is ready for her to present to the regional sales managers at their next meeting.

Tutorial Assignments

After Sally meets with the regional sales managers for MSI, she decides it would be a good idea to provide the managers with their own copy of the sales comparison worksheet, so they can update the report with next year's sales data, and also modify it to use for their own sales tracking purposes. Before passing it on to them, she wants to provide more documentation, and add some additional information that the managers thought would be useful to them. Complete the following for Sally:

1. Start Windows and Excel, if necessary. Insert your Student Disk into the appropriate disk drive. Make sure the Excel and Book1 windows are maximized.

2. Open the workbook MSI1 in the TAssign folder for Tutorial 2 on your Student Disk.

3. Save your workbook as MSI Sales Report 2 in the TAssign folder for Tutorial 2 on your Student Disk.

4. Make Sheet2 the active sheet. Use Sheet2 to include information about the workbook. Insert the information in Figure 2-34 into Sheet2. Increase the width of column A as necessary.

Excel

Figure 2-34 ◀

Cell	Text Entry
A1	Motorcycle Specialties Incorporated
A3	Created By:
A4	Date created:
A6	Purpose:
B3	enter your name
B4	enter today's date
B6	Sales report comparing sales by region for 1999 with 1998

5. Change the name of the worksheet from Sheet2 to Title Sheet.

6. Print the Title Sheet sheet.

7. Make Sales Comparison the active sheet.

 8. Open the Office Assistant and enter the search phrase "Insert a column" to obtain instruction on inserting a new column into a worksheet. Insert a new column between columns C and D.

9. In cell D4 enter the heading "Change."

10. In cell D5 enter the formula to calculate the change in sales for North America from 1998 to 1999. (*Hint*: Check that the figure in cell D5 is 50670.)

11. Copy the formula in D5 to the other regions and total (D6 through D9) using the fill handle.

12. Calculate summary statistics for 1998. In cell C13 display the average sales, in cell C14 display the maximum, and in cell C15 display the minimum.

13. Save the workbook.

14. Print the sales comparison worksheet.

 15. a. Use the Office Assistant to learn how to attach comments to a cell. List the steps.
   b. Insert the following comment into cell F4: "Divide 1999 sales in each region by total sales in 1999."

 16. Open the MSI3 workbook and save it as MSI Report 4.
   a. Use the AutoSum button to compute the totals for 1998 and 1999. Print the worksheet. Are the results correct?
   b. Replace the values in the range B5:C8 with "1". Print the worksheet. Are the results correct? Why do you think this problem occurred?
   c. Use the pointing method to correct the formula. Print the worksheet.

17. a. Use the Office Assistant to learn how to use row and column headers in your formulas to create formulas (enter the search phrase "labels as formulas").
    b. Open the MSI5 workbook and save it as MSI Report 6.
    c. In cell D5, calculate the change in sales in North America from 1998 to 1999 using the labels in columns B and C.
    d. Copy the formula in D5 to the other regions and total (D6 through D9) using the fill handle.
    e. Print the worksheet.
    f. Print the formulas.
    g. Save the worksheet.

18. Open the MSI7 workbook and save it as MSI Report 8.
    a. Activate the Sales Comparison sheet and select the range A1:E9. Copy the selected range to the Clipboard. Activate Sheet2 and paste the selected range to the corresponding cells in Sheet2. Apply the Classic 1 AutoFormat to this range. Print Sheet2.
    b. Insert a new sheet using the Worksheet command from the Insert menu. Return to the Sales Comparison sheet and copy the range A1:E9 to the corresponding cells in the new sheet. Apply the 3D Effects 2 AutoFormat to this range. Print this sheet.
    c. Use the Delete Sheet command from the Edit menu to delete the Title Sheet sheet.
    d. Move the Sales Comparison sheet so it is the third sheet in the workbook.
    e. Save the workbook.

Case Problems

1. Magazine Circulation Report You are a research analyst in the marketing department of a large magazine publisher. You have been assigned the task of compiling circulation data on the company's competition. Circulation statistics for the top six magazines appear in Figure 2-35.

Figure 2-35 ◀

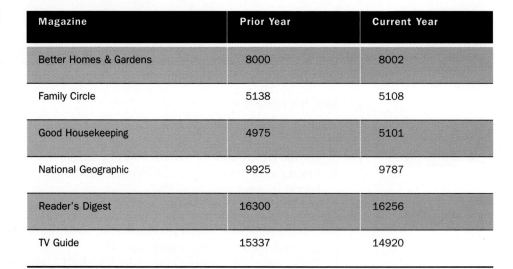

Magazine	Prior Year	Current Year
Better Homes & Gardens	8000	8002
Family Circle	5138	5108
Good Housekeeping	4975	5101
National Geographic	9925	9787
Reader's Digest	16300	16256
TV Guide	15337	14920

1. Open a new workbook and enter the data from Figure 2-35 in a worksheet.

2. Use the AutoSum button to compute total circulation for all six magazines listed for both the current year and the prior year.

3. Use the Paste Function dialog box to compute the average circulation for all six magazines for both the current and the prior year.

4. For each magazine, create and enter a formula to compute the increase/decrease in circulation compared to the prior year.

5. Use AutoFormat to improve the appearance of the worksheet. Use Classic 1 as the format.

6. Rename the sheet Total Circulation.

7. Use a sheet in the workbook to enter your name, the date created, and the purpose of this sheet. Rename the sheet Title Sheet.

8. Save the worksheet as Magazine in the Case folder for Tutorial 2.

9. Print both the worksheets.

2. Compiling Data on the U.S. Airline Industry The editor of *Aviation Week and Space Technology* has asked you to research the current status of the U.S. airline industry. You collect information on the revenue-miles and passenger-miles for each major U.S. airline (Figure 2-36).

Figure 2-36 ◄

Revenue-Miles and Passenger-Miles for Major U.S. Airlines		
Airline	Revenue-Miles (in 1000s of miles)	Passenger-Miles (in 1000s of miles)
American	26851	2210871
Continental	9316	622543
Delta	21515	1862276
Northwest	20803	1924288
US Air	9855	1542800
Trans World	16228	1188124
United	35175	3673152

You want to calculate the following summary information to use in the article:

- total revenue-miles for the U.S. airline industry
- total passenger-miles for the U.S. airline industry
- each airline's share of the total revenue-miles
- each airline's share of the total passenger-miles
- average revenue-miles for U.S. airlines
- average passenger-miles for U.S. airlines

Complete these steps:

1. Open a new workbook and enter the labels and data from Figure 2-36.

2. In cell A2, insert a second line to the title that reads:

   Compiled by: *XXXX*

   where *XXXX* is your name.

3. Enter the formulas to compute the total and average revenue-miles and passenger-miles. Use the SUM and AVERAGE functions where appropriate. Remember to include row labels to describe each statistic.

4. Add a column to display each airline's share of the total revenue-miles. Remember to include a column heading. You decide the appropriate location for this data.

5. Add a column to display each airline's share of the total passenger-miles. Remember to include a column heading. You decide the appropriate location for this data.

6. Name the worksheet Mileage Data.

7. Save the worksheet as Airline in the Case folder for Tutorial 2.

8. Print the worksheet. Center the report, no gridlines, and place the date in the upper-right corner of the header.

9. Select an AutoFormat to improve the appearance of your output.

10. Save your workbook.

11. Print the worksheet, centered on the page, no gridlines or row and column headings.

12. Print the formulas for the worksheet. Include row and column headings in the output.

3. Fresh Air Sales Incentive Program Carl Stambaugh is assistant sales manager at Fresh Air Inc., a manufacturer of outdoor and expedition clothing. Fresh Air sales representatives contact retail chains and individual retail outlets to sell the Fresh Air line.

This year, to spur sales, Carl has decided to run a sales incentive program for sales representatives. Each sales representative has been assigned a sales goal 15% higher than his or her total sales last year. All sales representatives who reach this new goal will be awarded an all-expenses-paid trip for two to Cozumel, Mexico.

Carl wants to track the results of the sales incentive program with an Excel worksheet. He has asked you to complete the worksheet by adding the formulas to compute:

■ actual sales in 1999 for each sales representative

■ sales goal in 1999 for each sales representative

■ percent of goal reached for each sales representative

He also wants a printout before he presents the worksheet at the next sales meeting. Complete these steps:

1. Open the workbook Fresh (in the Case folder for Tutorial 2 on your Student Disk). Maximize the worksheet window and save the workbook as Fresh Air Sales Incentives in the Case folder for Tutorial 2.

2. Complete the worksheet by adding the following formulas:
   a. 1999 Actual for each employee = Sum of Actual Sales for each quarter
   b. Goal 1999 for each employee = 1998 Sales X (1 + Goal % increase)
   c. % Goal reached for each employee = 1999 Actual / 1999 Goal

   (*Hint:* Use the Copy command. Review relative versus absolute references.)

3. Make the formatting changes using an AutoFormat to improve the appearance of the worksheet.

4. Print the worksheet, centered horizontally and vertically, and add an appropriate header. Add your name and date in the footer.

5. At the bottom of the worksheet (three rows after the last sales rep) add the average, maximum, and minimum statistics for columns C through I.

6. Save the workbook.

7. Print the worksheet.

8. As you scroll down the worksheet, the column headings no longer appear on the screen, making it difficult to know what each column represents. Use the Help system to look up "Freezing Panes." Implement this feature in your worksheet. Save the workbook. Explain the steps you take to freeze the panes.

4. Stock Portfolio for Juan Cortez   Your close friend, Juan Cortez, works as an accountant at a local manufacturing company. While in college, with a double major in accounting and finance, Juan dabbled in the stock market and expressed an interest in becoming a financial planner and running his own firm. To that end, he has continued his professional studies in the evenings with the aim of becoming a certified financial planner. He has already begun to provide financial planning services to a few clients. Because of his hectic schedule as a full-time accountant, part-time student taking evening classes, and part-time financial planner with client visits on the weekends, Juan finds it difficult to keep up with the data processing needs for his clients. You have offered to assist him until he completes his studies for the certified financial planner exams.

Juan asks you to set up a worksheet to keep track of a stock portfolio for one of his clients.

Open a new workbook and do the following:

1. Figure 2-37 shows the data you will enter into the workbook. For each stock, you will enter the name, number of shares purchased, and purchase price. Periodically, you will also enter the current price of each stock so Juan can review the changes with his clients.

2. In addition to entering the data, you need to make the following calculations:
   a. Cost = No of shares * Purchase price
   b. Current Value = No of shares * Current price
   c. Gains/Losses = Current value minus Cost
   d. Totals for Cost, Current value, and Gains/Losses

   Enter the formulas to calculate the Cost, Current Value, Gains/Losses, and Totals.

3. Save the workbook as Portfolio in the Case folder for Tutorial 2.

Figure 2-37 ◀

Stock	No. Of Shares	Purchase Price	Cost	Current Price	Current Value	Gains/ Losses
PepsiC	100	50.25		52.50		
FordM	250	31		30		
AT&T	50	60		61.25		
IBM	100	90.25		95.75		
Xerox	50	138		134		
Total						

4. Print the worksheet. Center the worksheet horizontally and vertically. Add an appropriate header.

5. Apply an AutoFormat that improves the appearance of the worksheet. Save the worksheet as Portfolio 2. Print the worksheet.

6. Print the formulas for the worksheet. Include row and column headings in the printed output.

7. Clear the prices in the Current price column of the worksheet.

8. Enter the following prices:

    PepsiC   55
    FordM   29.5
    AT&T   64
    IBM   91.25
    Xerox   125

    Print the worksheet.

9. From the financial section of your newspaper, look up the current price of each stock (all these stocks are listed on the New York Stock Exchange). Enter these prices in the worksheet. Print the worksheet.

Developing a Professional-Looking Worksheet

Producing a Projected Sales Report for the Pronto Salsa Company

OBJECTIVES

In this tutorial you will:

■ Format data using the Number, Currency, and Percentage formats

■ Align cell contents

■ Center text across columns

■ Change fonts, font style, and font size

■ Use borders and color for emphasis

■ Add comments and graphics to a worksheet using the Drawing toolbar

■ Remove gridlines from the worksheet

■ Print in landscape orientation

CASE

Pronto Salsa Company

Anne Castelar owns the Pronto Salsa Company, a successful business located in the heart of Tex-Mex country. She is working on a plan to add a new product, de Chili Guero Medium, to Pronto's gourmet salsa line.

Anne wants to take out a bank loan to purchase additional food-processing equipment to handle the production increase the new salsa requires. She has an appointment with her bank loan officer at 2:00 this afternoon. To prepare for the meeting, Anne creates a worksheet to show the projected sales of the new salsa and the expected effect on profits. Although the numbers and formulas are in place on the worksheet, Anne has no time to format the worksheet for the best impact. She planned to do that now, but an unexpected problem with today's produce shipment requires her to leave the office for a few hours. Anne asks you to complete the worksheet. She shows you a printout of the unformatted worksheet and explains that she wants the finished worksheet to look very professional—like those you see in business magazines. She also asks you to make sure that the worksheet emphasizes the profits expected from sales of the new salsa.

SESSION

3.1

In this session you will learn how to make your worksheets easier to understand through various formatting techniques. You will format values using Currency formats, Number formats, and Percentage formats. You will also change font styles and font sizes, and change the alignment of data within cells and across columns. As you perform all these tasks, you'll find the Format Painter button an extremely useful tool.

Opening the Workbook

After Anne leaves, you develop the worksheet plan in Figure 3-1 and the worksheet format plan in Figure 3-2.

Figure 3-1 ◀
Planning
analysis sheet

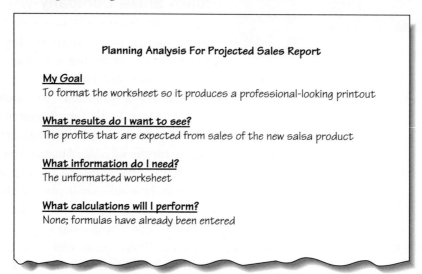

Planning Analysis For Projected Sales Report

My Goal
To format the worksheet so it produces a professional-looking printout

What results do I want to see?
The profits that are expected from sales of the new salsa product

What information do I need?
The unformatted worksheet

What calculations will I perform?
None; formulas have already been entered

Figure 3-2 ◀
Format plan

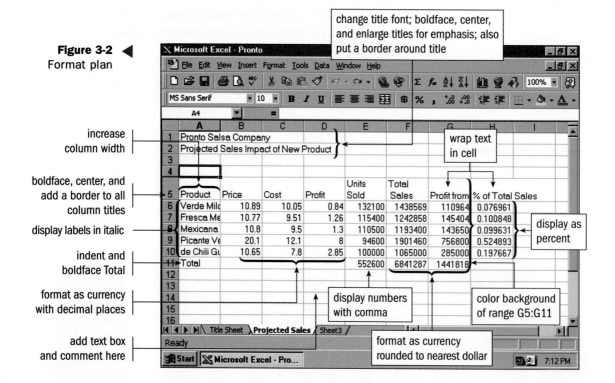

Anne has already entered all the formulas, numbers, and labels. Your main task is to format this information so it is easy to read and understand, and appears professional. This can be accomplished on two levels—by formatting the detailed data in the worksheet and by enhancing the appearance of the worksheet as a whole.

On the data level, you decide that the numbers should be formatted according to their use. For example, the product prices need to appear as dollar values. Secondly, the column and row labels need to fit within their cells. Also, the labels need to stand out more. To enhance the worksheet as a whole, you need to structure it so that related information is visually grouped together using lines and borders. Anne also wants certain areas of the worksheet that contain key information to stand out, and color may be a useful tool for this.

With all that needs to be done before Anne's 2:00 meeting, you decide that the best place to begin is with formatting the data within the worksheet. Once that is done, you will work to improve the worksheet's overall organization and appearance.

Now that the planning is done, you are ready to start Excel and open the workbook of unformatted data that Anne created.

To start Excel and organize your desktop:

1. Start Excel as usual.

2. Make sure your Student Disk is in the appropriate disk drive.

3. Make sure the Microsoft Excel and Book1 windows are maximized.

Now you need to open Anne's file and begin formatting the worksheet. Anne stored the workbook as Pronto, but before you begin to change the workbook, save it using the filename Pronto Salsa Company. This way, the original workbook, Pronto, remains unchanged in case you want to work through this tutorial again.

To open the Pronto workbook and save the workbook as Pronto Salsa Company:

1. Click the **Open** button 🖼 on the Standard toolbar to display the Open dialog box.

2. Open the **Pronto** workbook in the Tutorial.03 folder on your Student Disk.

3. Click **File** on the menu bar, and then click **Save As** to display the Save As dialog box.

4. In the File name text box, change the filename to **Pronto Salsa Company**.

5. Click the **Save** button to save the workbook under the new filename. The new filename, Pronto Salsa Company, appears in the title bar.

   TROUBLE? If you see the message "Replace existing file?" click the Yes button to replace the old version of Pronto Salsa Company with your new version.

6. Click the **Projected Sales** sheet tab. See Figure 3-3.

Figure 3-3 ◀
Pronto Salsa
Company
workbook

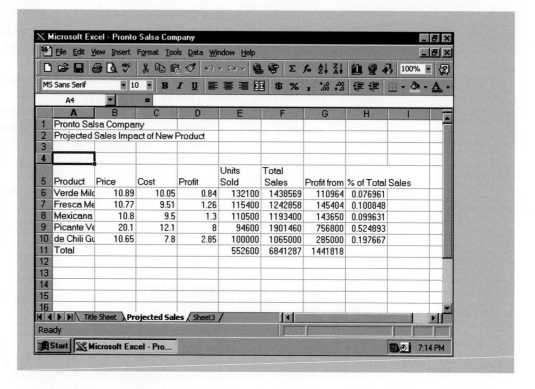

Studying the worksheet, you notice that the salsa names do not fit in column A. It is easy to widen column A, but if you do, some of the worksheet will scroll off the screen. Other formatting tasks are easier if you can see the entire worksheet, so you decide to do these tasks first.

Formatting Worksheet Data

Formatting is the process of changing the appearance of the data in worksheet cells. Formatting can make your worksheets easier to understand, and draw attention to important points.

In the previous tutorial you used AutoFormat to improve the appearance of your worksheet. AutoFormat applies a predefined format to your entire workbook. AutoFormat is easy to use, but its predefined format might not suit every worksheet. If you decide to customize a workbook's format, you can use the extensive Excel formatting options. When you select your own formats, you can format an individual cell or a range of cells.

Formatting changes only the appearance of the worksheet; it does not change the text or numbers stored in the cells. For example, if you format the number .123653 using a Percentage format that displays only one decimal place, the number appears in the worksheet as 12.4%; however, the original number, .123653, remains stored in the cell. When you enter data into cells, Excel applies an automatic format, referred to as the General format. The **General format** aligns numbers at the right side of the cell, uses a minus sign for negative values, and displays numbers without trailing zeros to the right of the decimal point. You can change the General format by using AutoFormat, the Format menu, the Shortcut menu, or toolbar buttons.

There are many ways to access the Excel formatting options. The Format menu provides access to all formatting commands. See Figure 3-4.

Excel

Figure 3-4 ◀
Format menu

The Shortcut menu provides quick access to the Format dialog box. See Figure 3-5. To display the Shortcut menu, make sure the pointer is positioned within the range you have selected to format, and then click the right mouse button.

Figure 3-5 ◀
Shortcut menu

The Formatting toolbar contains formatting buttons, including the style and alignment buttons, and the Font Style and Font Size boxes. See Figure 3-6.

Figure 3-6 ◀
Formatting
toolbar buttons

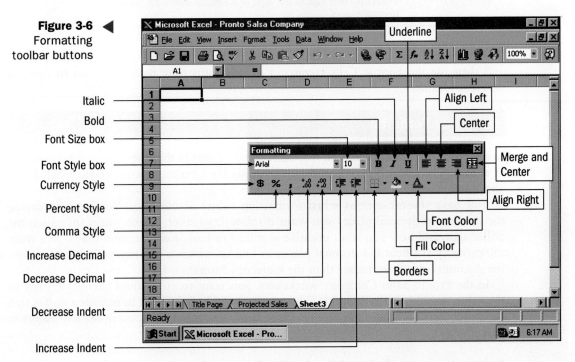

Most experienced Excel users develop a preference for which menu or buttons they use to access the Excel formatting options; however, most beginners find it easy to remember that all formatting options are available from the Format menu.

Looking at Anne's worksheet, you decide to change the appearance of the data first.

Changing the Appearance of Numbers

When the data in the worksheet appears as numbers, you want each number to appear in a style appropriate for what it is representing. The Excel default General format is often not the most appropriate style. For example, dollar values may require the dollar symbol ($) and thousand markers, and these can be applied to numerical data simply by changing the data's format. You can also standardize the number of decimal places displayed in a cell through formatting. Excel has a variety of predefined number formats. Figure 3-7 describes some of the most commonly used formats.

Figure 3-7 ◀
Commonly used
number formats

Category	Display Option
General	Excel default Number format; displays numbers without dollar signs, commas, or trailing decimal places
Number	Sets decimal places, negative number display, and comma separator
Currency	Sets decimal places and negative number display, and inserts dollar signs and comma separators
Accounting	Specialized monetary value format used to align dollar signs, decimal places, and comma separators
Date	Sets date or date and time display
Percentage	Inserts percent sign to the right of a number with a set number of decimal places

To change the number formatting, you select the cell or range of cells to be reformatted, and then use the Format Cells command or the Formatting toolbar button to apply a different format.

Currency Formats

In reviewing Anne's unformatted worksheet, you recognize that there are several columns of data that reflect currency. You decide to apply the Currency format to the Cost, Price, and Profit columns.

You have several options when formatting values as currency. You need to decide the number of decimal places you want displayed; whether or not you want to see the dollar sign; and how you want negative numbers to look. Keep in mind that if you want the currency symbols and decimal places to line up within a column, you should choose the Accounting format, rather than the Currency format.

In the Pronto Salsa Company worksheet, you want to apply the Currency format to the values in columns B, C, and D. The numbers will be formatted to include a dollar sign with two decimal places. You also decide to display negative numbers in the worksheet in parentheses.

To format columns B, C, and D using the Currency format:

1. Select the range **B6:D10**.

2. Click **Format** on the menu bar, and then click **Cells** to display the Format Cells dialog box.

3. If necessary, click the **Number** tab. See Figure 3-8.

Figure 3-8 ◀
Number tab of
Format Cells
dialog box

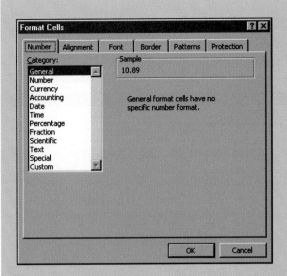

4. Click **Currency** in the Category list box. The Number tab changes to display the Currency formatting options, as shown in Figure 3-9. Notice that a sample of the selected format appears near the top of the dialog box. As you make further selections, the sample automatically changes to reflect your choices.

Figure 3-9 ◀
Selecting a
Currency
format

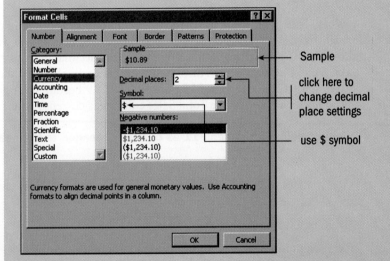

Sample

click here to
change decimal
place settings

use $ symbol

Notice that 2 decimal places is the default setting. A dollar sign ($) appears in the Symbol list box, indicating that the dollar sign will be displayed. If you are using a different currency, click the down arrow in the Symbol list box to select the currency symbol you want to display. Given the current options selected, you only need to select a format for negative numbers.

5. Click the third option **($1,234.10)** in the Negative numbers list box.

6. Click the **OK** button to format the selected range.

7. Click any cell to deselect the range and view the new formatting. See Figure 3-10.

Figure 3-10 ◀
Currency
formats in
columns B, C,
and D

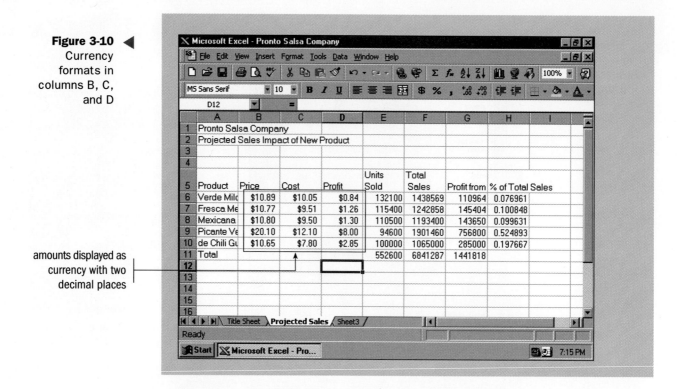

amounts displayed as
currency with two
decimal places

When your worksheet has large dollar amounts, you might want to use a Currency format that does not display any decimal places. To do this you use the Decrease Decimal button on the Formatting toolbar, or change the decimal places setting in the Format Cells dialog box. Currency values displayed with no decimal places are rounded to the nearest dollar: $15,612.56 becomes $15,613; $16,507.49 becomes $16,507; and so on.

You decide to format the Total Sales column as currency rounded to the nearest dollar.

To format cells F6 through F11 as currency rounded to the nearest dollar:

1. Select the range **F6:F11**.

2. Click **Format** on the menu bar, and then click **Cells** to display the Format Cells dialog box.

3. If necessary, click the **Number** tab.

4. Click **Currency** in the Category list box.

5. Click the **Decimal places** spin box down arrow twice to change the setting to 0 decimal places. Notice that the sample format changes to reflect the new settings.

6. Click the **OK** button to apply the format. Notice that Excel automatically increased the column width to display the formatted numbers.

7. Click any cell to deselect the range.

After formatting the Total Sales figures in column F, you realize you should have used the same format for the numbers in column G. To save time, you simply copy the formatting from column F to column G.

The Format Painter Button

The Format Painter button on the Standard toolbar lets you copy formats quickly from one cell or range to another. You simply click a cell containing the formats you want to copy, click the Format Painter button, and then use the click-drag technique to select the range to which you want to apply the copied formats.

Excel

To copy the format from cell F6:

1. Click cell **F6** because it contains the format you want to copy.

2. Click the **Format Painter** button ⌧ on the Standard toolbar. As you move the pointer over the worksheet cells, notice that the pointer turns to ✛🖌.

3. Position ✛🖌 over cell G6, and then click and drag to select cells **G6:G11**. When you release the mouse button, the cells appear in the Currency format, rounded to the nearest dollar—the same format used in cells F6 through F11.

4. Click any cell to deselect the range and view the formatted Profit from Sales column. See Figure 3-11.

Figure 3-11 ◀
Worksheet
after Format
Painter used to
copy formats

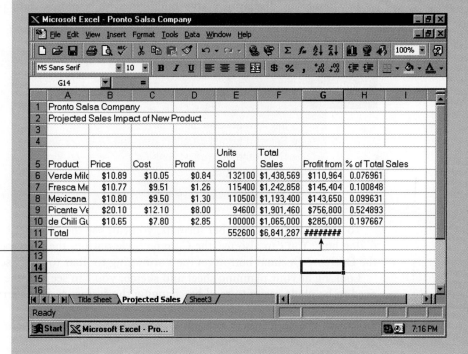

number symbols
indicate column width
needs to increase

As you review the changes on the screen, you notice that cell G11 contains number symbols (######) instead of values. This is because the formatting change has caused the data to exceed the width of the cell.

Number Symbol (###) Replacement

If a number is too long to fit within a cell's boundaries, Excel displays a series of number symbols (###) in the cell. The number symbols indicate that the number of digits in the value exceeds the cell's width. The number or formula is still stored in the cell, but the current cell width is not large enough to display the value. To display the value, you just need to increase the column width. One way you can do this is to use the Shortcut menu.

To replace the number symbols by increasing the column width:

1. Position the pointer on the column heading for column G.

2. Right-click the mouse button to display the Shortcut menu.

3. Click **Column Width** to display the Column Width dialog box.

4. Type **9** in the Column Width box.

5. Click the **OK** button to view the total sales, $1,441,818.

6. Click any cell to view the formatted data.

Now the cells containing price, cost, profit, total sales, and profit from sales are formatted as currency. Next, you want to apply formats to the numbers in columns E and H so that they are easier to read.

Number Formats

Like Currency formats, the Excel Number formats offer many options. You can select Number formats to specify

- the number of decimal places displayed
- whether to display a comma to delimit thousands, millions, and billions
- whether to display negative numbers with a minus sign, parentheses, or red numerals

REFERENCE window

FORMATTING NUMBERS

- Select the cells you want the new format applied to.
- Click Format, click Cells, and then click the Numbers tab in the Format Cells dialog box.
- Select a format category from the Category list box.
- Select the desired options for the selected format.
- Click the OK button.

To access all Excel Number formats, you can use the Number tab in the Format Cells dialog box. You can also use the Comma Style button, the Increase Decimal button, and the Decrease Decimal button on the Formatting toolbar to select some Number formats.

Looking at your planning sheet and sketch, you can see that the numbers in column E need to be made easier to read by changing the format to include commas.

To format the contents in column E with a comma and no decimal places:

1. Select the range **E6:E11**.

2. Click the **Comma Style** button ⬚ on the Formatting toolbar to apply the Comma Style. The default for the Comma Style is to display numbers with two places to the right of the decimal. Use the Decrease Decimal button ⬚ on the Formatting toolbar to decrease the number of decimal places displayed in cells formatted with the Comma Style to zero.

3. Click the **Decrease Decimal** button ⬚ on the Formatting toolbar twice to display the number with no decimal places.

4. Click any cell to deselect the range and view the formatted Units Sold column. See Figure 3-12.

Figure 3-12
Cells formatted
with Number
format

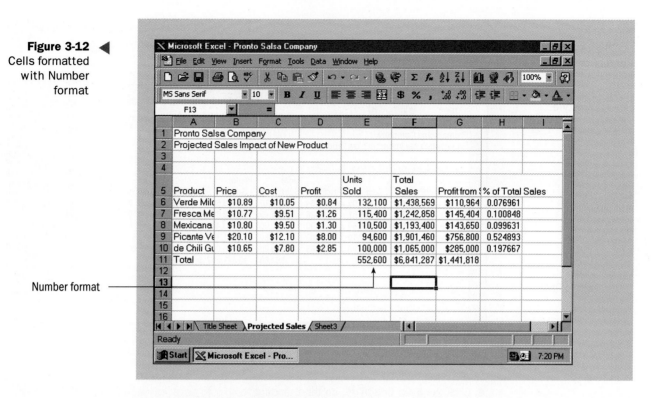

Number format

Looking at the numbers in column H, you realize that they are difficult to interpret and decide that you do not need to display so many decimal places. What are your options for displaying percentages?

Percentage Format

When formatting values as percentages, you need to select how many decimal places you want displayed. The Percentage format with no decimal places displays the number 0.18037 as 18%. The Percentage format with two decimal places displays the same number as 18.04%. If you want to use the Percentage format with two decimal places, you select this option using the Number tab in the Format Cells dialog box. You can also use the Percent Style button on the Formatting toolbar, and then click the Increase Decimal button twice to add two decimal places.

Your format sketch specifies a Percentage format with no decimal places for the values in column H. You could use the Number tab to choose this format. But it's faster to use the Percent Style button on the Formatting toolbar.

To format the values in column H as a percentage with no decimal places:

1. Select the range **H6:H10.**

2. Click the **Percent Style** button ![%] on the Formatting toolbar.

3. Click any cell to deselect the range and view the Percent Style. See Figure 3-13.

Figure 3-13 ◀
Percent of total
sales formatted
with Percent
Style

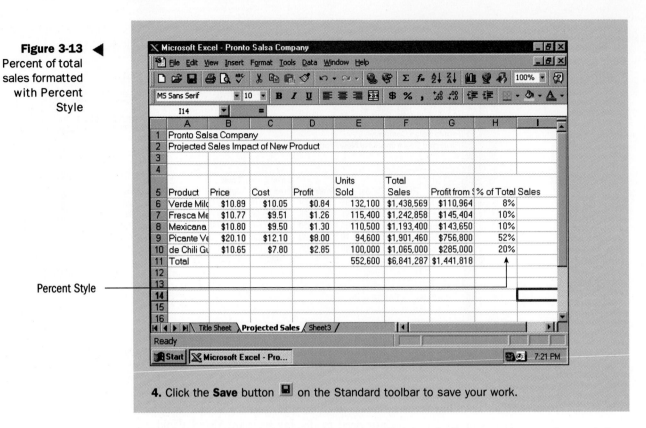

Percent Style

4. Click the **Save** button 🖫 on the Standard toolbar to save your work.

You review the worksheet. You have now formatted all the numbers in the worksheet appropriately. The next step in formatting Anne's worksheet is to improve the alignment of the data in the cells.

Aligning Cell Contents

The **alignment** of data in a cell is the position of the data relative to the right and left edges of the cell. Cell contents can be aligned on the left or right side of the cell, or centered in the cell. When you enter numbers and formulas, Excel automatically aligns them on the cell's right side. Excel automatically aligns text entries on the cell's left side. The default Excel alignment does not always create the most readable worksheet. Figure 3-14 shows a worksheet with the column titles left-aligned and the numbers in the columns right-aligned.

Figure 3-14 ◀
Poorly
formatted
worksheet

column titles
left-aligned

numbers
right-aligned

Notice how difficult it is to figure out which numbers go with each column title. Centering or right-aligning column titles would improve the readability of the worksheet in Figure 3-14. As a general rule, you should center column titles, format columns of numbers so that the decimal places are in line, and leave columns of text aligned on the left. You can change the alignment of cell data using the four alignment tools on the Formatting toolbar, or you can access additional alignment options by selecting the Alignment tab in the Format Cells dialog box.

To center the column titles:

1. Select the range **A5:H5**.

2. Click the **Center** button ▤ on the Formatting toolbar to center the cell contents.

3. Click any cell to deselect the range and view the centered titles. See Figure 3-15.

Figure 3-15 ◀
Worksheet with
centered
column titles

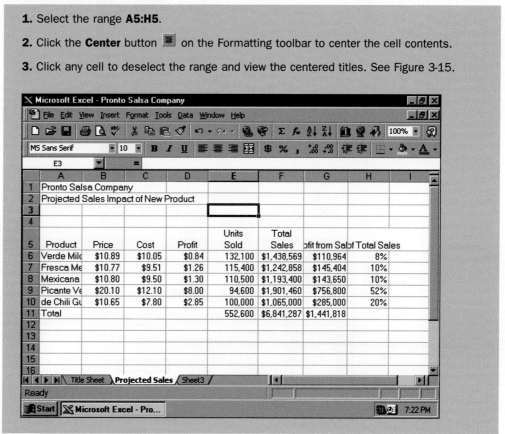

Notice that the column titles in columns G and H are not fully displayed. Although you could widen the column widths of these two columns to display the entire text, the Excel Wrap Text option enables you to display a label within a cell.

Wrapping Text in a Cell

As you know, if you enter a label that's too wide for the active cell, Excel extends the label past the cell border and into the adjacent cells—provided those cells are empty. If you select the Wrap Text option, Excel will display your label entirely within the active cell. To accommodate the label, the height of the row in which the cell is located is increased, and the text is "wrapped" onto the additional lines.

Now wrap the column titles in columns G and H.

To wrap text within a cell:

1. Select the range **G5:H5**.

2. Click **Format** on the menu bar, and then click **Cells** to display the Format Cells dialog box.

3. Click the **Alignment** tab. See Figure 3-16.

Figure 3-16 ◀
Alignment tab
of Format Cells
dialog box

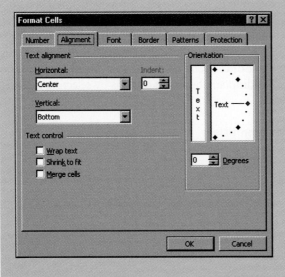

4. Click the **Wrap text** check box in the Text control area to select that option.

5. Click the **OK** button to apply the text wrapping.

6. Click any cell to deselect the range and view the entire text displayed in the cell. See Figure 3-17.

Figure 3-17 ◀
Wrapping text
in a cell

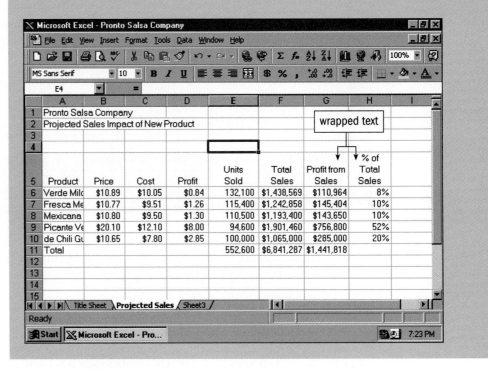

Now you will center the main worksheet titles.

Centering Text Across Columns

Sometimes you might want to center a cell's contents across more than one column. This is particularly useful for centering titles at the top of a worksheet. Now you will use the Center Across Selections option from the Format Cells dialog box to center the worksheet titles in cells A1 and A2 across columns A through H.

Excel

To center the worksheet titles across columns A through H:

1. Select the range **A1:H2**.

2. Click **Format**, click **Cells**, and if necessary click the **Alignment** tab in the Format Cells dialog box.

3. Click the arrow next to the Horizontal text alignment list box to display the horizontal text alignment options.

4. Click the **Center Across Selection** option to center the title lines across columns A through H.

5. Click the **OK** button.

6. Click any cell to deselect the range. See Figure 3-18.

Figure 3-18 ◀
Worksheet with titles centered across several columns

cell contents centered across columns A through H

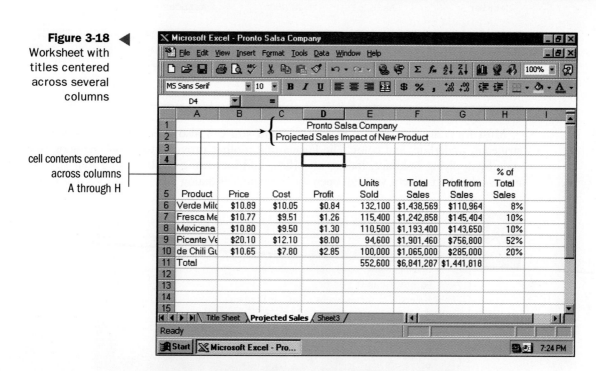

Indenting Text Within a Cell

When you type text in a cell it is left-aligned. You can indent text from the left edge by using the Increase Indent button on the Formatting toolbar or the Index spinner button in the Alignment tab of the Format Cells dialog box. You decide to indent the word "Total" to provide a visual cue of the change from detail to summary information.

To indent text within a cell:

1. Click cell **A11** to make it the active cell.

2. Click the **Increase Indent** button 🔳 on the Formatting toolbar to indent the word "Total" within the cell.

3. Click the **Save** button 🔳 on the Standard toolbar to save the worksheet.

You check your plan and confirm that you selected formats for all worksheet cells containing data, and that the data within the cells is aligned properly. The formatting of the worksheet contents is almost complete. Your next task is to improve the appearance of the labels by changing the font style of the title and the column headings.

You decide to use the Bold button on the Formatting toolbar to change some titles in the worksheet to boldface.

Changing the Font, Font Style, and Font Size

A **font** is a set of letters, numbers, punctuation marks, and symbols with a specific size and design. Figure 3-19 shows some examples. A font can have one or more of the following **font styles**: regular, italic, bold, and bold italic.

Figure 3-19 ◀
Selected fonts

Font	Regular Style	Italic Style	Bold Style	Bold Italic Style
Times	AaBbCc	AaBbCc	**AaBbCc**	*AaBbCc*
Courier	AaBbCc	AaBbCc	**AaBbCc**	*AaBbCc*
Garamond	AaBbCc	*AaBbCc*	**AaBbCc**	*AaBbCc*
Helvetica Condensed	AaBbCc	*AaBbCc*	**AaBbCc**	*AaBbCc*

Most fonts are available in many sizes, and you can also select font effects, such as strikeout, underline, and color. The Formatting toolbar provides tools for changing font style by applying boldface, italics, underline, and increasing or decreasing font size. To access other font effects, you can open the Format Cells dialog box from the Format menu.

REFERENCE window

CHANGING FONT, FONT STYLE, AND FONT SIZE

- Select the cells you want the new format to apply to.
- Click Format, click Cells, and then click the Font tab in the Format Cells dialog box.
- Select a typeface from the Font list box.
- Select a font style from the Font style list box.
- Select a type size from the Size list box.
- the OK button.
  or
- Select the cells you want the new format to apply to.
- Select the font, font size, and font style using the buttons on the Formatting toolbar.

You begin by formatting the word "Total" in cell A11 in boldface letters.

To apply the boldface font style:

1. If necessary, click cell **A11**.

2. Click the **Bold** button **B** on the Formatting toolbar to set the font style to boldface. Notice that when a style like bold is applied to a cell's content, the toolbar button appears depressed to indicate that the style is applied to the active cell.

You also want to display the column titles in boldface. To do this, first select the range you want to format, and then click the Bold button to apply the format.

To display the column titles in boldface:

1. Select the range **A5:H5**.

2. Click the **Bold** button ⬛ on the Formatting toolbar to apply the boldface font style.

3. Click any cell to deselect the range.

Next, you decide to display the salsa products' names in italics.

To italicize the row labels:

1. Select the range **A6:A10**.

2. Click the **Italic** button ⬛ on the Formatting toolbar to apply the italic font style.

3. Click any cell to deselect the range and view the formatting you have done so far. See Figure 3-20.

Figure 3-20 ◀
Bold and Italic
formats applied

bold

italic

text indented

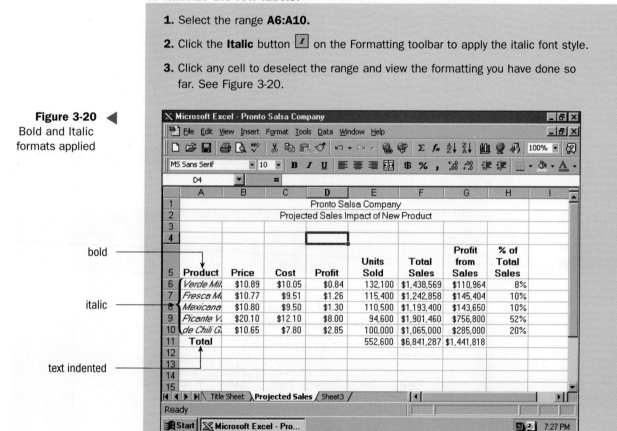

Next, you want to change the font and size of the worksheet titles for emphasis. You use the Font dialog box (instead of the toolbar) so you can preview your changes. Remember, although the worksheet titles appear to be in columns A through F, they are just spilling over from column A. To format the titles, you need to select only cells A1 and A2—the cells where the titles were originally entered.

To change the font and font size of the worksheet titles:

1. Select the range **A1:A2**.

2. Click **Format** on the menu bar, and then click **Cells** to display the Format Cells dialog box.

3. Click the **Font** tab. See Figure 3-21.

Figure 3-21 ◀
Font tab in
Format Cells
dialog box

select new
font here

change font
size here

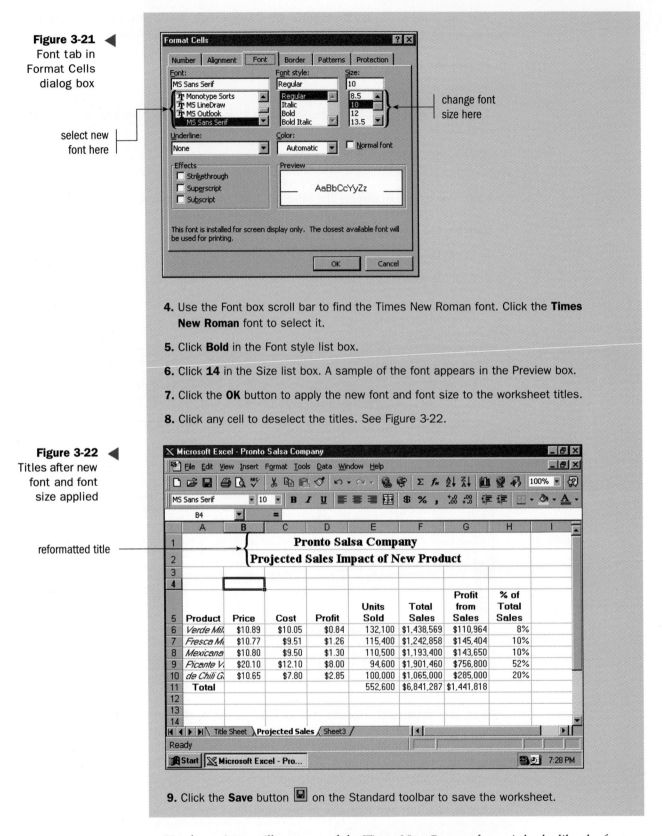

4. Use the Font box scroll bar to find the Times New Roman font. Click the **Times New Roman** font to select it.

5. Click **Bold** in the Font style list box.

6. Click **14** in the Size list box. A sample of the font appears in the Preview box.

7. Click the **OK** button to apply the new font and font size to the worksheet titles.

8. Click any cell to deselect the titles. See Figure 3-22.

Figure 3-22 ◀
Titles after new
font and font
size applied

reformatted title

9. Click the **Save** button 🖫 on the Standard toolbar to save the worksheet.

You hope Anne will approve of the Times New Roman font—it looks like the font on the Pronto salsa jar labels.

Quick Check

1 | If the number .128912 is in a cell, what will Excel display if you:
  a. Format the number using the Percentage format with no decimal places
  b. Format the number using the Currency format with 2 decimal places and the dollar sign

2 | List three ways you can access formatting commands, options, and tools.

3 | Explain why Excel might display 3,045.39 in a cell, but 3045.38672 in the formula bar.

4 | List the options available on the Formatting toolbar for aligning data.

5 | What are the general rules you should follow for aligning column headings, numbers, and text labels?

6 | Explain two ways to completely display a label that currently is not entirely displayed.

7 | The _____ copies formats quickly from one cell or range to another.

8 | A series of ####### in a cell indicates _____.

Now that you have finished formatting the data in the worksheet, you need to enhance the worksheet's appearance and readability as a whole. You will do this in Session 3.2 by applying borders, colors, and a text box.

SESSION 3.2

In this session you learn how to enhance a worksheet's overall appearance by adding borders and color. You will use the Drawing toolbar to add a text box and graphic to the worksheet, and use landscape orientation to print the worksheet.

Adding and Removing Borders

A well-constructed worksheet is clearly divided into zones that visually group related information. Figure 3-23 shows the zones on your worksheet. Lines, called **borders**, can help to distinguish different zones of the worksheet and add visual interest.

Figure 3-23 ◀
Information
zones

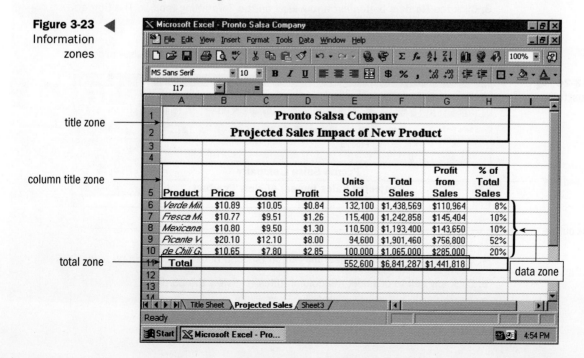

You can create lines and borders using either the Borders button on the Formatting toolbar, or the Border tab in the Format Cells dialog box. You can place a border around a single cell or a group of cells using the Outline option. To create a horizontal line, you place a border at the top or bottom of a cell. To create a vertical line, you place a border on the right or left side of a cell.

The Border tab lets you choose from numerous border styles, including different line thicknesses, double lines, dashed lines, and colored lines. With the Borders button, your choice of border styles is more limited.

To remove a border from a cell or group of cells, you can use the Border tab in the Format Cells dialog box. To remove all borders from a selected range of cells, select the None button in the Presets area.

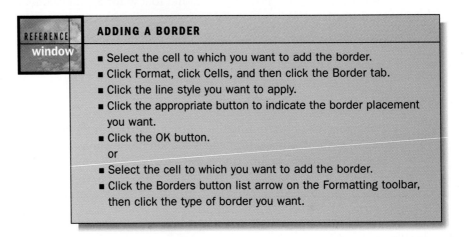

REFERENCE window

ADDING A BORDER

- Select the cell to which you want to add the border.
- Click Format, click Cells, and then click the Border tab.
- Click the line style you want to apply.
- Click the appropriate button to indicate the border placement you want.
- Click the OK button.
  or
- Select the cell to which you want to add the border.
- Click the Borders button list arrow on the Formatting toolbar, then click the type of border you want.

You decide that a thick line under all column titles will separate them from the data in the columns. To do this, you use the Borders button on the Formatting toolbar.

To underline column titles:

1. If you took a break after the last session, make sure Excel is running and the Projected Sales worksheet of the Pronto Salsa Company workbook is open.

2. Select the range **A5:H5**.

3. Click the **Borders** button list arrow on the Formatting toolbar. The Borders palette appears. See Figure 3-24.

Figure 3-24 ◄
Borders palette

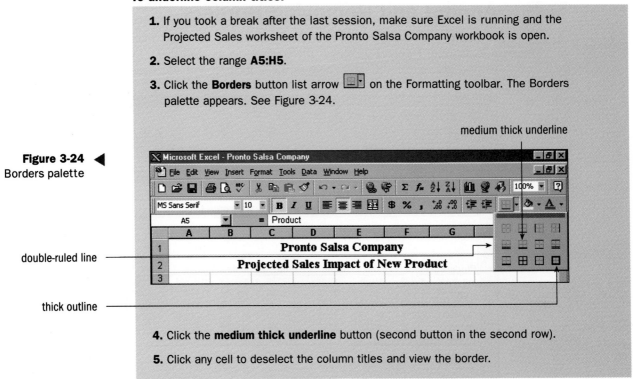

medium thick underline

double-ruled line

thick outline

4. Click the **medium thick underline** button (second button in the second row).

5. Click any cell to deselect the column titles and view the border.

You also want a line to separate the data from the totals in row 11, and a double-ruled line below the totals. This time you use the Border tab in the Format Cells dialog box to apply borders to cells.

To add a line separating the data and the totals and a double-ruled line below the totals:

1. Select the range **A11:H11**.

2. Click **Format** on the menu bar, click **Cells**, and then click the **Border** tab in the Format Cells dialog box. See Figure 3-25.

Figure 3-25 ◀
Border tab from
Format Cells
dialog box

applies selected line
style to top border

applies selected line
style to bottom border

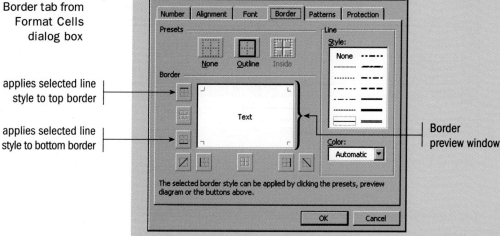

Border
preview window

3. Click the **medium thick line** in the Line Style box (third from the bottom in the second column).

4. Click the **top border** button. A thick line appears at the top of the Border preview window.

5. Click the **double-ruled line** in the Line Style box.

6. Click the **bottom border** button. A double-ruled line appears at the bottom of the Border preview window.

7. Click the **OK** button to apply the borders.

8. Click any cell to deselect the range and view the borders. See Figure 3-26.

Figure 3-26 ◀
Borders applied
to worksheet

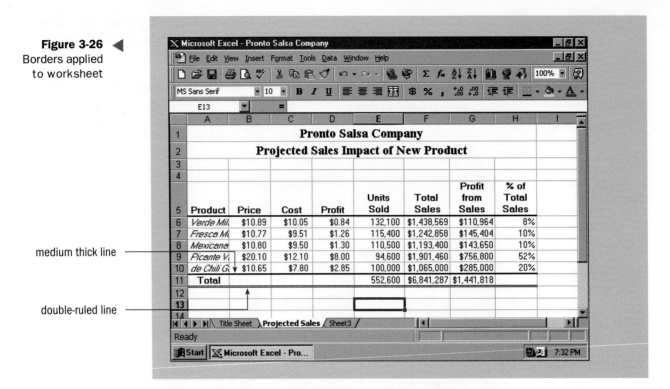

medium thick line

double-ruled line

You consult your format sketch and see that you planned a border around the title zone to add a professional touch. You decide to add this border next.

To place an outline border around the title zone:

1. Select the range **A1:H2**.

2. Click the **Borders** button list arrow [icon] on the Formatting toolbar to display the Borders palette.

3. Click the **thick outline** button in the last row.

4. Click any cell to deselect the titles and view the border.

5. Click the **Save** button [icon] on the Standard toolbar to save the worksheet.

In addition to a border around the title zone, you want to add color to emphasize the Profit from Sales column.

Using Color for Emphasis

Patterns and colors provide visual interest, emphasize worksheet zones, or indicate data-entry areas. You should base the use of patterns or colors on the way you intend to use the worksheet. If you print the worksheet in color and distribute a hard copy of it, or if you plan to use a color projection device to display your worksheet on screen, you can take advantage of the Excel color formatting options. If you do not have a color printer, you can use patterns. It is difficult to predict how colors you see on your screen will be translated into gray shades on your printout.

APPLYING PATTERNS AND COLOR

- Select the cells you want to fill with a pattern or color.
- Click Format, click Cells, and then click the Patterns tab in the Format Cells dialog box.
- Select a pattern from the Pattern drop-down list. If you want the pattern to appear in a color, select a color from the Pattern palette, too.
- If you want a colored background, select it from the Cell shading color palette. You can also select colors by clicking the Color button on the Formatting toolbar and then clicking the color you want.

You want your worksheet to look good when you print it in black and white on the office laser printer, but you also want it to look good on the screen when you show it to Anne. You decide that a yellow background will enable the Profit from Sales column to stand out and looks fairly good on the screen and the printout. You apply this format using the Patterns tab in the Format Cells dialog box.

To apply a color to the Profit from Sales column:

1. Select the range **G5:G11**.

2. Click **Format** on the menu bar, click **Cells,** and then click the **Patterns** tab in the Format Cells dialog box. See Figure 3-27.

Figure 3-27 ◀
Color palette in
the Patterns
tab of the
Format Cells
dialog box

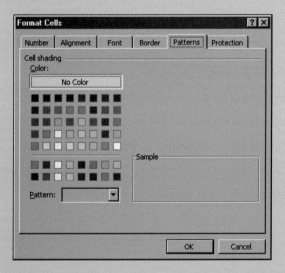

3. Click the **yellow square** in the fourth row (third square from the left) of the Cell shading Color palette.

4. Click the **OK** button to apply the color.

5. Click any cell to deselect the range and view the color in the Profit from Sales column. See Figure 3-28.

Figure 3-28 ◀
Worksheet
after applying
color to
a column

yellow background ——

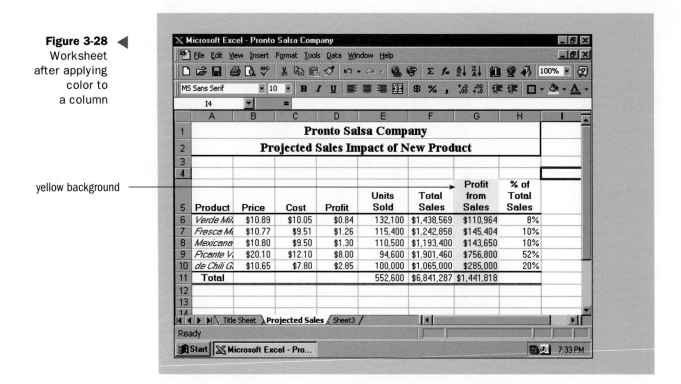

You delayed changing the width of column A because you knew that doing so would cause some columns to scroll off the screen, forcing you to scroll around the worksheet to format all the labels and values. Now that you have finished formatting labels and values, you can change the width of column A to best display the information in that column. To do this, you can use the Shortcut menu to change the column width.

To change the column width using the Shortcut menu:

1. Position the pointer on the column heading for column A.

2. Right-click the mouse button to display the Shortcut menu.

3. Click **Column Width** to display the Column Width dialog box.

4. Type **25** in the Column Width text box.

5. Click the **OK** button.

6. Click any cell to deselect the column and view the results of the column width change. See Figure 3-29.

Figure 3-29 ◄
Results of
changing
column width

column width
increased to 25

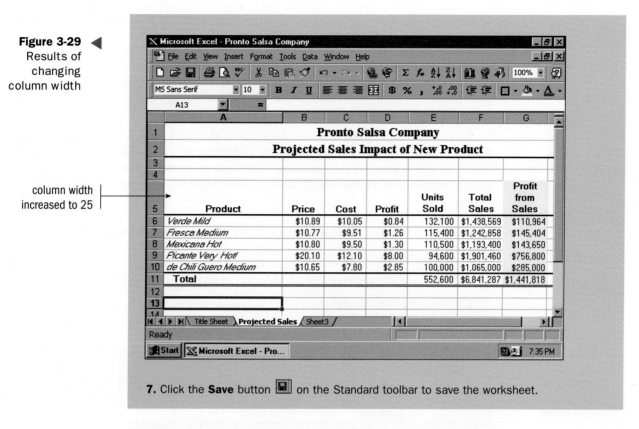

7. Click the **Save** button 🔲 on the Standard toolbar to save the worksheet.

Adding Comments to the Worksheet

The Excel Text Box feature lets you display a comment in a worksheet. A comment is like an electronic Post-It note that you paste inside a rectangular text box in the worksheet.

To add a comment to your worksheet, you first create a text box, then you simply type the text in the box. You create a text box using the Text Box button, which is located on the Drawing toolbar.

Activating a Toolbar

Excel provides many toolbars. You have been using two: the Standard toolbar and the Formatting toolbar. Some of the other toolbars include the Chart toolbar, the Drawing toolbar, and the Visual Basic toolbar. To activate a toolbar, it's usually easiest to use the toolbar Shortcut menu, but to activate the Drawing toolbar you can simply click the Drawing button on the Standard toolbar. When you finish using a toolbar, you can easily remove it from the worksheet.

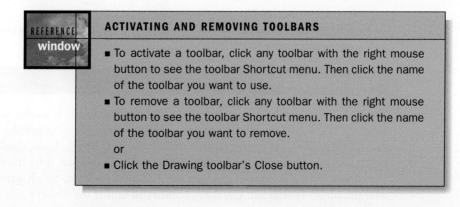

REFERENCE
window

ACTIVATING AND REMOVING TOOLBARS

■ To activate a toolbar, click any toolbar with the right mouse button to see the toolbar Shortcut menu. Then click the name of the toolbar you want to use.

■ To remove a toolbar, click any toolbar with the right mouse button to see the toolbar Shortcut menu. Then click the name of the toolbar you want to remove.
or

■ Click the Drawing toolbar's Close button.

You need the Drawing toolbar to accomplish your next formatting task. (If your Drawing toolbar is already displayed, skip the following step.)

To display the Drawing toolbar:

1. Click the **Drawing** button on the Standard toolbar.

The toolbar might appear in any location in the worksheet window; this is called a **floating toolbar**. You don't want the toolbar obstructing your view of the worksheet, so drag it to the bottom of the worksheet window, to **anchor** it there. (If your toolbar is already anchored at the bottom of the worksheet window, or at the top, skip the next set of steps.)

To anchor the Drawing toolbar to the bottom of the worksheet window:

1. Position the pointer on the title bar of the Drawing toolbar.

2. Click and drag the toolbar to the bottom of the screen.

3. Release the mouse button to attach the Drawing toolbar to the bottom of the worksheet window. See Figure 3-30.

Figure 3-30 ◄
Drawing toolbar attached to bottom of window

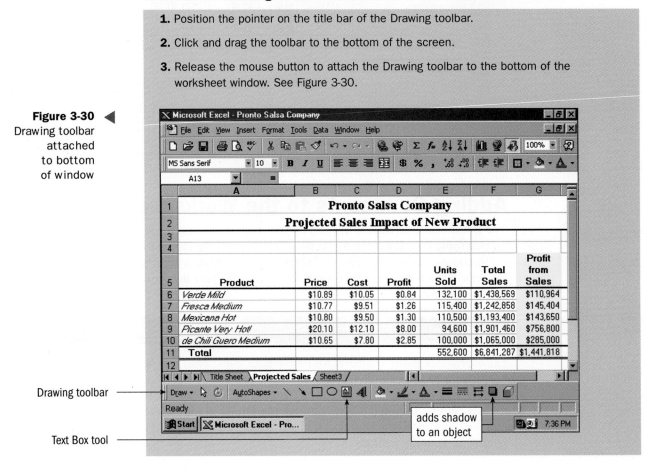

Drawing toolbar

Text Box tool

Now that the Drawing toolbar is where you want it, you proceed with your plan to add a comment to the worksheet.

Adding a Text Box

A **text box** is a block of text that sits in the worksheet. It is useful for adding comments to worksheets and charts. The text box is one example of a graphic object. With Excel you can create a variety of graphic objects, such as boxes, lines, circles, arrows, and text boxes. To move, modify, or delete an object, you first select it by moving the pointer over the object until the pointer changes to ▹ , then clicking. Small square handles indicate that the object is selected. Use these handles to adjust the object's size, change its location, or delete it.

Excel

REFERENCE window

ADDING A TEXT BOX AND COMMENT

- Click the Text Box button on the Drawing toolbar.
- Position the pointer where you want the text box to appear in the worksheet.
- Click and drag to outline the size and shape of the text box.
- Type the comment text for the text box.
- Click any cell outside the text box when you complete the comment.

You want to draw attention to the new salsa product's low price and high profit margin. To do this, you plan to add a text box to the bottom of the worksheet that contains a comment about expected profits.

To add a comment in a text box:

1. Scroll the worksheet so you can see rows 7 through 21.

2. Click the **Text Box** button 📧 on the Drawing toolbar. As you move the pointer inside the worksheet area, the pointer changes to ↓. Position the crosshair of the pointer at the top of cell **A13** to mark the upper-left corner of the text box.

3. Click and drag ✛ to cell **C18**, and then release the mouse button to mark the lower-right corner of the text box. See Figure 3-31.

   You are ready to type the text into the text box.

Figure 3-31 ◄
Creating a
text box

text box →

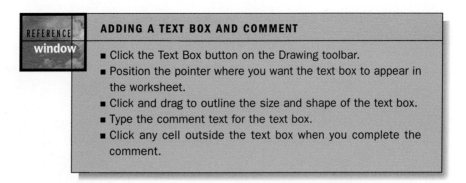

4. Make sure the insertion point is in the text box and then type **Notice the low cost and high profit margin of the de Chili Guero Medium. It has the lowest cost, the lowest price, and the second highest profit per unit.**

You want to use a different font style to emphasize the name of the new salsa product in the text box.

To italicize the name of the new salsa product:

1. Position I in the text box just before the word "de Chili."

2. Click and drag I to the end of the word "Medium", and then release the mouse button.

   TROUBLE? Don't worry if the text in your text box is not arranged exactly like the text in the figure. If the size of your text box differs slightly from the one in the figure, the lines of text might break differently.

3. Click the **Italic** button *I* on the Formatting toolbar.

4. Click any cell to deselect the product name, which now appears italicized. See Figure 3-32.

Figure 3-32 ◄
Italicizing text
in the text box

italicized text ——

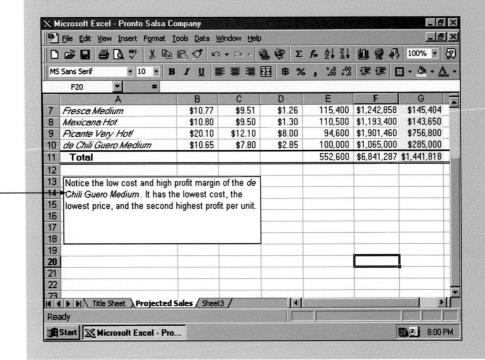

You decide to change the text box size so that there is no empty space at the bottom.

To change the text box size:

1. Click the **text box** to select it and display the patterned border with handles.

2. Position the pointer on the center handle at the bottom of the text box. The pointer changes to ↕ .

3. Click and drag ↕ up to shorten the box, and then release the mouse button.

You want to change the text box a bit more by adding a drop shadow to it.

To add a shadow to the text box:

1. Make sure the text box is still selected. (Look for the patterned border and handles.)

2. Click the **Shadow** button ▢ on the Drawing toolbar to display the gallery of Shadow options. See Figure 3-33.

Figure 3-33 ◀
Shadow
style options

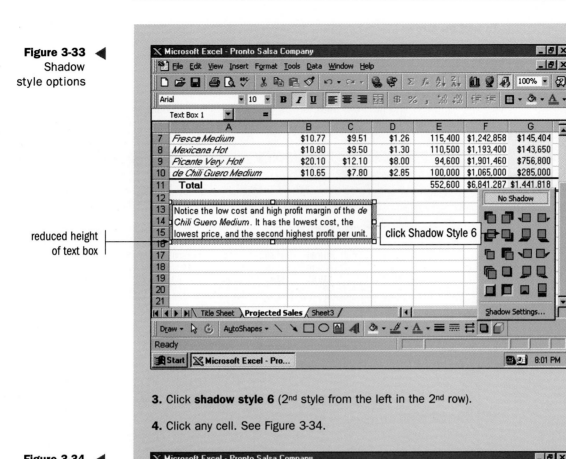

reduced height
of text box

3. Click **shadow style 6** (2nd style from the left in the 2nd row).

4. Click any cell. See Figure 3-34.

Figure 3-34 ◀
Text box
with shadow

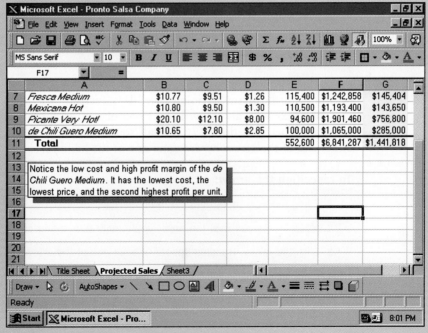

Adding an Arrow

You decide to add an arrow pointing from the text box to the row with information on the new salsa.

To add an arrow:

1. Click the **Arrow** button ![arrow button] on the Drawing toolbar. As you move the mouse pointer inside the worksheet, the pointer changes to +.

2. Position + on the top edge of the text box in cell **B12**. To ensure a straight line, press and hold the **Shift** key as you drag + to cell **B10**, and then release the mouse button. See Figure 3-35.

Figure 3-35 ◄
Creating
an arrow

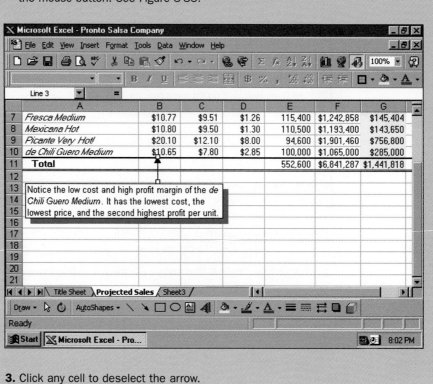

3. Click any cell to deselect the arrow.

You want the arrow to point to cell D10 instead of B10, so you need to reposition it. Like a text box, an arrow is an Excel object. To modify the arrow object, you must select it. When you do so, two small square handles appear on it. You can reposition either end of the arrow by dragging one of the handles.

To reposition the arrow:

1. Scroll the worksheet until row 5 appears as the first visible row in the window.

2. Move the pointer over the arrow object until the pointer changes to ✛.

3. Click the **arrow**. Handles appear at each end of the arrow.

4. Move the pointer to the top handle on the arrowhead until the pointer changes to ↖.

5. Click and drag + to cell **D10**, and then release the mouse button.

6. Click any cell to deselect the arrow object. See Figure 3-36.

Figure 3-36 ◄
Moving
the arrow

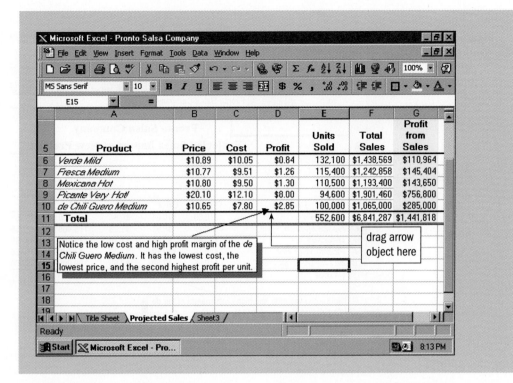

Now that the text box is finished, you can remove the Drawing toolbar from the worksheet.

To remove the Drawing toolbar:

1. Click the **Drawing** button 🖉 on the Standard toolbar. The Drawing toolbar is removed from the window, and the Drawing button 🖉 no longer appears depressed (selected).

2. Press **Ctrl + Home** to make cell A1 the active cell.

3. Click the **Save** button 🖫 on the Standard toolbar to save your work.

You have now made all the formatting changes and enhancements to Anne's worksheet. She has just returned to the office, and you show her the completed worksheet. She is very pleased with how professional the worksheet looks, but she thinks of one more way to improve the appearance of the worksheet. She asks you to remove the gridlines from the worksheet display.

Controlling the Display of Gridlines

Although normally the boundaries of each cell are outlined in black, Anne has decided that the appearance of your worksheet will be more effective if you remove the display of gridlines. To remove the gridline display, you deselect the Gridlines option in the View tab of the Options dialog box.

To remove the display of gridlines in the worksheet:

1. Click **Tools** on the menu bar, click **Options**, and if necessary, click the **View** tab in the Options dialog box.

2. Click the **Gridlines** check box in the Window option to remove the check and deselect the option.

3. Click the **OK** button to display the worksheet without gridlines. See Figure 3-37.

Figure 3-37 ◄
Worksheet
without
gridlines

no gridlines

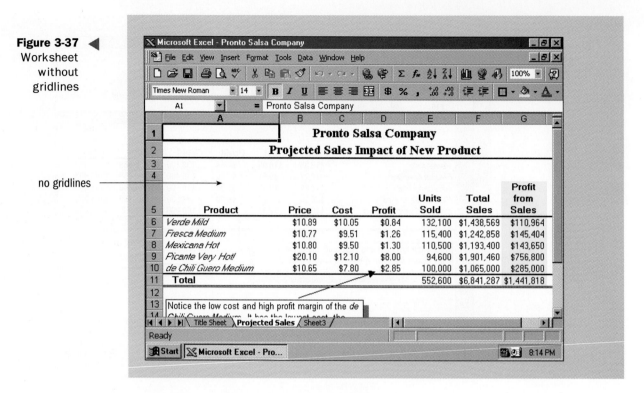

Now you are ready to print the worksheet.

Printing the Worksheet

Before you print a worksheet, you can use the Excel Print Preview window to see how it will look when printed. Recall that the Print Preview window shows you margins, page breaks, headers, and footers that are not always visible on the screen.

To preview the worksheet before you print it:

1. Click the **Print Preview** button 🔍 on the Standard toolbar to display the first worksheet page in the Print Preview window. See Figure 3-38.

Figure 3-38 ◄
Print Preview

active Next button
indicates more pages

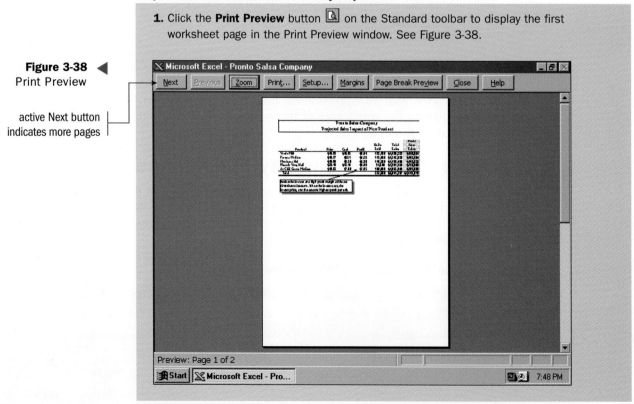

2. Click the **Next** button to preview the second worksheet page. Only one column appears on this page.

3. Click the **Previous** button to preview the first page again.

Looking at the Print Preview, you see that the worksheet is too wide to fit on a single page. You realize that if you print the worksheet lengthwise, however, it will fit on a single sheet of paper.

Portrait and Landscape Orientations

Excel provides two print orientations, portrait and landscape. **Portrait orientation** prints the worksheet with the paper positioned so it is taller than it is wide. **Landscape orientation** prints the worksheet with the paper positioned so it is wider than it is tall. Because some worksheets are wider than they are tall, landscape orientation is very useful.

You can specify print orientation using the Page Setup command on the File menu or using the Setup button in the Print Preview window. Use the landscape orientation for the Projected Sales worksheet.

To change the print orientation to landscape:

1. In the Print Preview window, click the **Setup** button to display the Page Setup dialog box. If necessary, click the **Page** tab.

2. Click the **Landscape** option button in the Orientation section to select this option.

3. Click the **OK** button to return to the Print Preview window. See Figure 3-39. Notice the Landscape orientation; that is, the page is wider than it is tall.

Figure 3-39 ◄
Landscape
orientation

Next button no
longer active

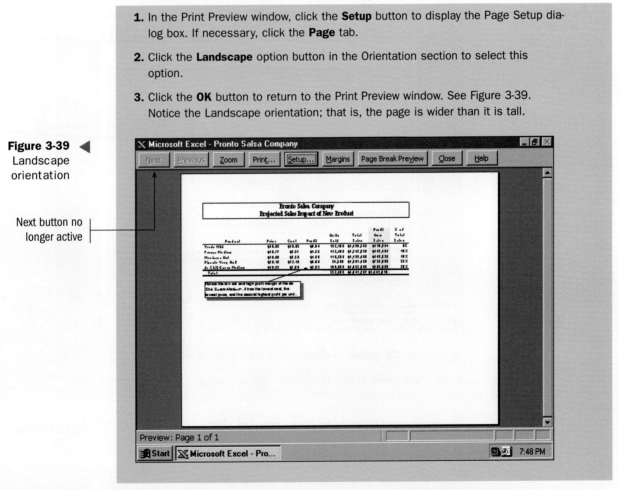

Before printing the worksheet, center the output on the page, and use the header/footer tab to document the printed worksheet.

To center the printed output:

1. Click the **Setup** button to display the Page Setup dialog box. Click the **Margins** tab.

2. Click the **Center on page Horizontally** check box to place a check in it and select that option.

Next, modify the printed footer by adding the date in the left section, and Anne's name in the right section.

To change the worksheet footer:

1. Click the **Header/Footer** tab, and then click the **Custom footer** to display the Footer dialog box.

2. In the Left section box, click the **Date** button 📅 to display &Date in the Left section box.

3. Click the **Right section** box, then type **Prepared by Anne Castelar.**

4. Click the **OK** button to complete the footer and return to the Page Setup dialog box. See Figure 3-40.

Figure 3-40 ◄
Page Setup
after changing
the footer

from right section
of Custom Footer
dialog box

from left section
of Custom Footer
dialog box

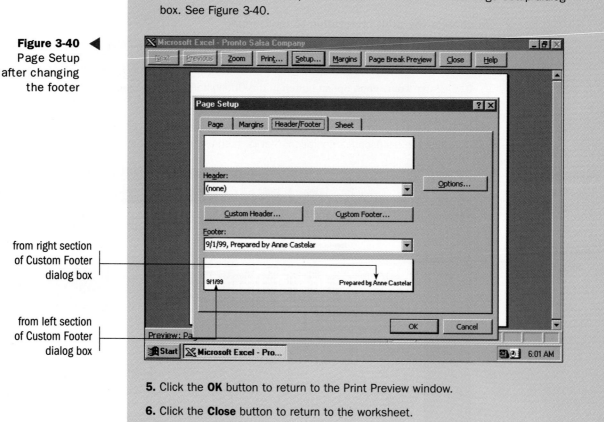

5. Click the **OK** button to return to the Print Preview window.

6. Click the **Close** button to return to the worksheet.

The worksheet is ready to print, but you always save your work before printing.

To save your page setup settings and print the worksheet:

1. Click the **Save** button 💾 on the Standard toolbar.

2. Click the **Print** button 🖨 on the Standard toolbar. The worksheet prints. See Figure 3-41.

TROUBLE? If you see a message that indicates that you have a printer problem, click the Cancel button to cancel the printout. Check your printer to make sure it is turned on and is online; also make sure it has paper. Then go back and try Step 2 again. If you have no printer available, click the Cancel button.

Figure 3-41 ◄
Printed
worksheet

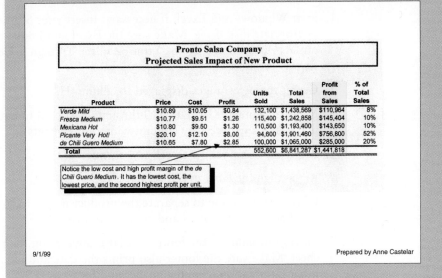

TROUBLE? If the title for the last two columns didn't print completely, you need to increase the row height for row 5. Select row 5. Drag the border below row 5 until the row height is 42.75 or greater (check the reference area of the formula bar). Click the Print button.

Now that you are done formatting the worksheet, close the workbook and exit Excel.

3. Close the workbook and exit Excel.

Quick Check

1 List two ways you can place a double-ruled line at the bottom of a range of cells.

2 Describe how to activate the Drawing toolbar.

3 To move, modify, or delete an object, you must _____ it first.

4 A _____ is a block of text that is placed in the worksheet.

5 _____ orientation prints the worksheet with the paper positioned so it is taller than it is wide.

6 If you are asked to remove the gridlines from the worksheet display, you will do what to the worksheet?

7 An arrow is an example of a _____.

You have completed formatting the Projected Sales worksheet and are ready to give it to Anne to check over before she presents it at her meeting with the bank loan officer.

Tutorial Assignments

After you show Anne the Projected Sales worksheet, the two of you discuss alternative ways to improve the worksheet's appearance. You decide to make some of these changes and give Anne the choice between two formatted worksheets. Do the following:

1. Start Windows and Excel, if necessary. Insert your Student Disk into the appropriate disk drive. Make sure the Excel and Book1 windows are maximized. Open the workbook Pronto2 in the TAssign folder for Tutorial 3 and save as Pronto3.

2. Center the percentages displayed in column H.

3. Make the contents of cells A10 through H10 bold to emphasize the new product. Make any necessary column-width adjustments.

4. Apply the color yellow to cells A1 through H2.

5. Right-align the label in cell A11.

6. Draw a vertical line to separate the product names from the rest of the data (the line begins in row 6 and continues to row 10).

7. Enter your name in the footer so that it appears on the printout of the worksheet. Make sure the footer also prints the date and filename. Remove any other information from the header and footer.

8. Make sure the Page Setup menu settings are set for centered horizontally and vertically, no row/column headings, and no cell gridlines.

9. Preview the printout to make sure it fits on one page. Save and print the worksheet.

 10. Fill the text box with the color yellow so that it appears as a "yellow sticky note."

 11. Change the color of the two-line title to red (the text, not the background color).

 12. In step 4 you applied the color yellow to the cells A1 through H2. Remove the yellow color so that the background is the same as the rest of your worksheet.

13. If you answered steps 10, 11, or 12, save the worksheet as Pronto4.

 14. a. Study the worksheet shown in Figure 3-42. Then open the Office Assistant and inquire about rotating and merging text in a cell.

Figure 3-42 ◀

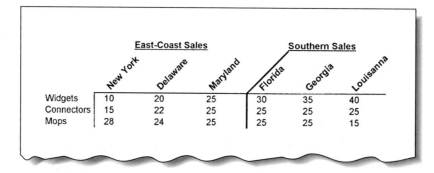

b. Open the workbook Explore3 and save it as Explore3 Solution.
c. Use the Rotate Text formatting feature to change the worksheet so it is similar to Figure 3-42. Make any other changes to make the worksheet as similar as possible to the one shown in Figure 3-42.
d. Save and print the worksheet.

Case Problems

1. Jenson Sports Wear Quarterly Sales Carl is the national sales manager for Jenson Sports Wear, a company that sells sports wear to major department stores. He has been using an Excel worksheet to track the results of a sales incentive program in which his sales staff has been participating. He has asked you to format the worksheet so it looks professional. He also wants a printout before he presents the worksheet at the next sales meeting. Complete these steps to format and print the worksheet:

1. Start Windows and Excel, if necessary. Insert your Student Disk into the appropriate disk drive. Make sure the Excel and Book1 windows are maximized. Open the workbook Running in the Case folder for Tutorial 3 on your Student Disk. Maximize the worksheet window and save the workbook as Running2 in the Case folder for Tutorial 3.

2. Complete the worksheet by doing the following:

   a. Calculating totals for each product
   b. Calculating quarterly subtotals for the Shoes and Shirts departments
   c. Calculating totals for each quarter and an overall total

3. Modify the worksheet so it is formatted as shown in Figure 3-43.

4. Use the Page Setup dialog box to center the output both horizontally and vertically.

5. Add the filename, your name, and the date in the footer section and delete the formatting code &[File] from the Center section of the header.

6. Save the worksheet.

7. Preview the worksheet and adjust the page setup as necessary for the printed results you want.

8. Print the worksheet.

9. Place the comment "Leading product" in a text box. Remove the border from the text box. (*Hint*: Use the Format Object dialog box.) Draw an oval object around the comment. (*Hint*: Use the Oval tool on the Drawing toolbar.) Draw an arrow from the edge of the oval to the number in the worksheet representing the leading product. Save and print the worksheet. Your printout should fit on one page.

Figure 3-43 ◀

Jenson Sports Wear
Quarterly Sales by Product

Shoes	Qtr 1	Qtr 2	Qtr 3	Qtr 4	Total
Running	1,750	2,050	2,125	2,200	8,125
Tennis	2,450	2,000	2,200	2,400	9,050
Basketball	1,150	1,300	1,450	1,500	5,400
Subtotal	5,350	5,350	5,775	6,100	22,575
Shirts	**Qtr 1**	**Qtr 2**	**Qtr 3**	**Qtr 4**	**Total**
Tee	900	1,100	1,000	1,050	4,050
Polo	2,000	2,100	2,200	2,300	8,600
Sweat	250	250	275	300	1,075
Subtotal	3,150	3,450	3,475	3,650	13,725
Total	8,500	8,800	9,250	9,750	36,300

2. Age Group Changes in the U.S. Population Rick Stephanopolous works for the U.S. Census Bureau and has been asked by his manager to prepare a report on changes in the U.S. population. Part of his report focuses on age group changes in the population from 1970 through 1980. Rick has created a worksheet that contains information from the U.S. Census reports from these years, and he is ready to format it. Complete these steps to format the worksheet:

1. Start Windows and Excel, if necessary. Insert your Student Disk into the appropriate disk drive. Make sure the Excel and Book1 windows are maximized. Open the workbook Census in the Case folder for Tutorial 3, and then save the workbook as US Population in the Case folder for Tutorial 3.

2. Make the formatting changes shown in Figure 3-44, adjusting column widths as necessary.

3. Use the Page Setup dialog box to modify the header so that the Right section consists of your name, a space, the current date, and the filename. Delete the contents of the Center section of the header.

4. Save the workbook.

5. Preview and print the worksheet. Your printout should fit on one page.

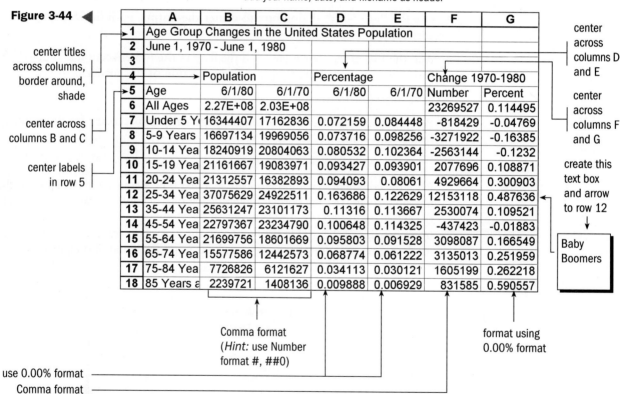

Figure 3-44

add your name, date, and filename as header

center titles across columns, border around, shade

center across columns B and C

center labels in row 5

center across columns D and E

center across columns F and G

create this text box and arrow to row 12

Baby Boomers

Comma format (*Hint:* use Number format #, ##0)

format using 0.00% format

use 0.00% format
Comma format

	A	B	C	D	E	F	G
1	Age Group Changes in the United States Population						
2	June 1, 1970 - June 1, 1980						
3							
4		Population		Percentage		Change 1970-1980	
5	Age	6/1/80	6/1/70	6/1/80	6/1/70	Number	Percent
6	All Ages	2.27E+08	2.03E+08			23269527	0.114495
7	Under 5 Y	16344407	17162836	0.072159	0.084448	-818429	-0.04769
8	5-9 Years	16697134	19969056	0.073716	0.098256	-3271922	-0.16385
9	10-14 Yea	18240919	20804063	0.080532	0.102364	-2563144	-0.1232
10	15-19 Yea	21161667	19083971	0.093427	0.093901	2077696	0.108871
11	20-24 Yea	21312557	16382893	0.094093	0.08061	4929664	0.300903
12	25-34 Yea	37075629	24922511	0.163686	0.122629	12153118	0.487636
13	35-44 Yea	25631247	23101173	0.11316	0.113667	2530074	0.109521
14	45-54 Yea	22797367	23234790	0.100648	0.114325	-437423	-0.01883
15	55-64 Yea	21699756	18601669	0.095803	0.091528	3098087	0.166549
16	65-74 Yea	15577586	12442573	0.068774	0.061222	3135013	0.251959
17	75-84 Yea	7726826	6121627	0.034113	0.030121	1605199	0.262218
18	85 Years a	2239721	1408136	0.009888	0.006929	831585	0.590557

EXPLORE

6. Change the border color of the text box from black to red. Change the color of the arrow to red. Save the workbook as US Population2. If you have access to a color printer, print the worksheet.

3. State Recycling Campaign Fred Birnbaum is working as an intern in the state's Waste Disposal Department. They have a pilot project on recycling for three counties (Seacoast, Metro, and Pioneer Valley). You have been asked to complete the worksheet and format it for presentation to their board of directors.

1. Start Windows and Excel, if necessary. Insert your Student Disk into the appropriate disk drive. Make sure the Excel and Book1 windows are maximized. Open the workbook Recycle in the Case folder on your Student Disk and save it as Recycle2.

2. Add two columns to calculate yearly totals for tons and a dollar value for each material in each county.

3. Insert three rows at the top of the worksheet to include:

   State Recycling Project
   Material Reclamation 1999
   <blank row>

4. Format the worksheet until you feel confident that the board of directors will be impressed with the appearance of the report.

5. Rename the worksheet Recycle Data.

6. Save the worksheet.

7. Print the worksheet centered horizontally and vertically on the page, using landscape orientation.

8. Remove the gridlines from the display. Use the Border tab of the Format Cells dialog box to place the recycle data, cells A6 to K20, in a grid. Save the workbook as Recycle3.

9. Change the magnification of the sheet so you can view the recycle data on the screen without having to scroll. (*Hint*: Use the Zoom control on the Standard toolbar.)

4. Cash Budgeting at Halpern's Appliances Fran Valence, the business manager for Halpern's Appliances, a small retail appliance store, is in the process of preparing a cash budget for January. The store has a loan that must be paid the first week in February. Fran wants to determine whether the business will have enough cash to make the loan payment to the bank.

Fran sketches the projected budget so that it will have the format shown in Figure 3-45.

Figure 3-45 ◄

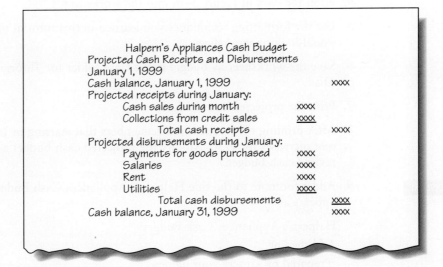

Do the following:

1. Start Windows and Excel, if necessary. Insert your Student Disk into the appropriate disk drive. Make sure the Excel and Book1 windows are maximized.

2. Use only columns A, B, and C to create the worksheet sketched in Figure 3-45.

3. Use the following formulas in your worksheet:

   a. Total cash receipts = Cash sales during month + Collections from credit sales
   b. Total cash disbursements = Payments for goods purchased + Salaries + Rent + Utilities
   c. Cash Balance, January 31, 1999 = Cash Balance, January 1, 1999 + Total cash receipts - Total cash disbursements

Figure 3-46 ◀

Budget Item	Amount
Cash balance at beginning of month	32000
Cash sales during month	9000
Collections from credit sales	17500
Payments for goods purchased	15000
Salaries	4800
Rent	1500
Utilities	800

4. Enter the data in Figure 3-46 into the worksheet.

5. Use the formatting techniques you learned in this tutorial to create a professional-looking worksheet.

6. Save the worksheet as Budget in the Case folder for Tutorial 3 on your Student Disk.

7. Print the projected cash budget.

8. After printing the budget Fran remembers that starting in January the monthly rent increases by $150. Modify the projected cash budget accordingly. Print the revised cash budget.

9. Add a footnote to the title Halpern's Appliances Cash Budget title line so it appears as

   Halpern's Appliances Cash Budget[1]
   Add the line
   [1]Prepared by <insert your name>

two rows after the last row. (*Hint*: Check out Superscript in the Font tab of the Format Cells dialog box.) Save the workbook as Budget1. Print the revised budget.

TUTORIAL 4

Creating Charts

Charting Sales Information for Cast Iron Concepts

CASE

Cast Iron Concepts

The regional sales manager of Cast Iron Concepts (CIC), a distributor of cast iron stoves, Andrea Puest, is required to present information on how well the company's products are selling within her territory. Andrea sells in the New England region, which currently includes Massachusetts, Maine, and Vermont. She sells four major models—Star Windsor, Box Windsor, West Windsor, and Circle Windsor. The Circle Windsor is CIC's latest entry in the cast iron stove market. Due to production problems it was only available for sale the last four months of the year.

Andrea will make a presentation before the Director of Sales for CIC and the other regional managers next week when the entire group meets at corporate headquarters. Andrea gives you the basic data on sales in her territory for the past year. She must report on how well each model is moving in total for the region as well as within each state she covers. She knows that this kind of information is often understood best when it is presented in graphical form. So, she thinks she would like to show this information in a column chart as well as in a pie chart. You will help her prepare for her presentation by creating the charts she needs.

SESSION

4.1

In this session you will learn about the variety of Excel chart types and learn to identify the elements of a chart. You will learn how to create a column chart and learn a number of techniques for improving your chart, including moving and resizing it, adding and editing chart text, enhancing a chart title by adding a border, and using color for emphasis.

Excel Charts

Andrea's sales data is saved in a workbook named Concepts. You will generate the charts from the data in this workbook.

To start Excel, open the Concepts workbook, and rename it:

1. Start Excel as usual.

2. Open the **Concepts** workbook in the Tutorial.04 folder on your Student Disk.

   The Title Sheet sheet appears as the first sheet in the workbook. You can type your name and the current date and then save the workbook under a new name.

3. Type your name and the current date in the appropriate cells in the Title Sheet sheet.

4. Save the workbook as **Cast Iron Concepts**. After you do so, the new filename appears in the title bar.

5. Click the **Sales Data** tab to move to that sheet. See Figure 4-1.

Figure 4-1 ◄
Sales Data
worksheet in
Cast Iron
Concepts
workbook

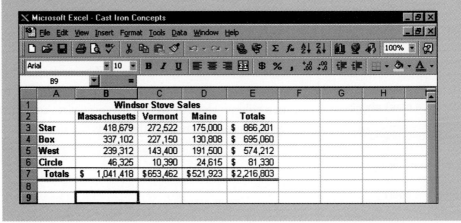

The worksheet shows the annual sales in dollars for each Windsor stove model by state. The total sales during the year for each model are in column E, and the total sales for each state appear in row 7.

It is easy to visually represent this kind of worksheet data. You might think of these graphical representations as "graphs"; however, in Excel they are referred to as **charts**. Figure 4-2 shows the 14 chart types within Excel that you can use to represent worksheet data.

Each chart type has two or more subtypes that provide various alternative charts for the selected chart type. For example, the Column chart type has seven subtypes, as shown in Figure 4-3. You can find more information on chart types and formats in the *Microsoft Excel User's Guide*, in the Excel Help facility, and in the Excel Chart Wizard.

Figure 4-2 ◀
Excel chart
types

Icon	Chart Type	Purpose
	Area	Shows magnitude of change over a period of time
	Column	Shows comparisons between the data represented by each column
	Bar	Shows comparisons between the data represented by each bar
	Line	Shows trends or changes over time
	Pie	Shows the proportion of parts to a whole
	XY (Scatter)	Shows the pattern or relationship between sets of (x,y) data points
	Radar	Shows change in data relative to a center point
	Surface chart	Shows the interrelationships between large amounts of data
	Bubble	A special type of XY (Scatter) that shows the pattern or relationship between sets of data points; compares three sets of data
	Stock	Compares high, low, open, and close prices of a stock
	Cylinder	Shows comparisons between the data represented by each cylinder
	Cone	Shows comparisons between the data represented by each cone
	Pyramid	Shows comparisons between the data represented by each pyramid
	Doughnut	Shows the proportion of parts to a whole

Figure 4-3 ◀
Chart subtypes
for Column
chart type

Chart Subtype Icon	Description
	Clustered column
	Stacked column
	100% Stacked column
	Clustered column with 3-D visual effect
	Stacked column with 3-D visual effect
	100% Stacked column with 3-D visual effect
	3-D column

Figure 4-4 shows the elements of a typical Excel chart. Understanding the Excel chart terminology is particularly important so you can successfully construct and edit charts.

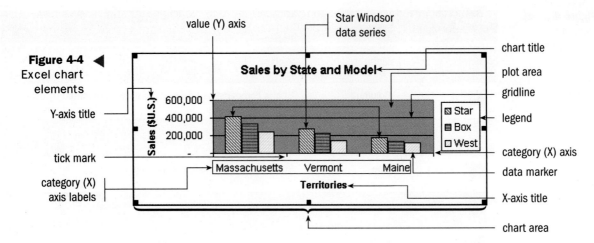

Figure 4-4
Excel chart
elements

The entire chart and all its elements are contained in the **chart area**. The **plot area** is the rectangular area defined by the axis, with the Y-axis forming the left side and the X-axis forming the base; in Figure 4-4 the plot area is in gray. The **axis** is a line that borders one side of the plot area, providing a frame for measurement or comparison in a chart. Data values are plotted along the **value** or **Y-axis**, which is typically vertical. Categories are plotted along the **category** or **X-axis**, which is usually horizontal. Each axis in a chart can have a title that identifies the scale or categories of the chart data; in Figure 4-4 the **X-axis title** is "Territories" and the **Y-axis title** is "Sales ($U.S.)." The **chart title** identifies the chart.

A **tick mark label** identifies the categories, values, or series in the chart. **Tick marks** are small lines that intersect an axis like divisions on a ruler, and represent the scale used for measuring values in the chart. Excel automatically generates this scale based on the values selected for the chart. **Gridlines** extend the tick marks on a chart axis to make it easier to see the values associated with the data markers. The **category names** or **category labels**, usually displayed on the X-axis, correspond to the labels you use for the worksheet data.

A **data point** is a single value originating from a worksheet cell. A **data marker** is a graphic representing a data point in a chart; depending on the type of chart, a data marker can be a bar, column, area, slice, or other symbol. For example, sales of the Star Windsor stove in Massachusetts (value 418,679 in cell B3 of the worksheet on your screen) is a data point. Each column in the chart in Figure 4-4 that shows the sales of Windsor stoves is a data marker. A **data series** is a group of related data points, such as the Star Windsor sales shown as red column markers in the chart.

When you have more than one data series, your chart will contain more than one set of data markers. For example, Figure 4-4 has three data series, one for each Windsor stove. When you show more than one data series in a chart, it is a good idea to use a **legend** to identify which data markers represent each data series.

Charts can be placed in the same worksheet as the data; this type of chart is called an **embedded chart**, and enables you to place the chart next to the data so it can easily be reviewed and printed on one page. You can also place a chart in a separate sheet, called a **chart sheet**, which contains only one chart and doesn't have rows and columns. In this tutorial you will create both an embedded chart and a chart that resides in a separate chart sheet.

Planning a Chart

Before you begin creating a chart you should plan it. Planning a chart includes the following steps:

- identifying the data points to be plotted, as well as the labels representing each data series and categories for the X-axis

- choosing an appropriate chart type

- sketching the chart, including data markers, axes, titles, labels, and legend

- deciding on the location of the chart within the workbook

Remember, Andrea wants to compare sales for each model in each state in which she sells. She thinks that a column chart is the best way to provide her audience with an accurate comparison of sales of Windsor stoves in her New England territory. She also needs to show how total sales in her territory are broken down by stove model. When showing parts of a whole, a pie chart is most effective, so she will create a pie chart to use in her presentation as well.

Andrea sketched the column chart and pie chart shown in Figure 4-5.

Figure 4-5 ◀
Sketch of
column and
pie charts

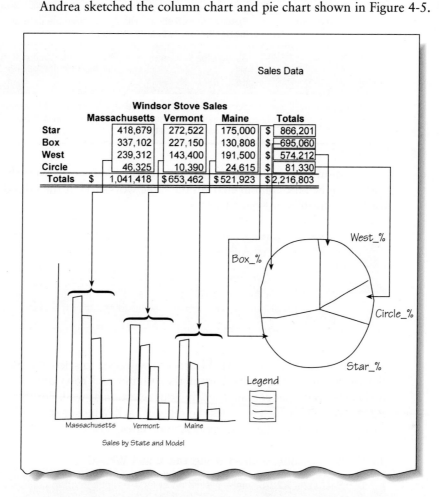

The sketches show roughly how Andrea wants the charts to look. It is difficult to envision exactly how a chart will look until you know how the data series looks when plotted; therefore, you don't need to incorporate every detail in the chart sketch. As you construct the charts, you can take advantage of Excel previewing capabilities to try different formatting options until your charts look just the way you want.

Create the column chart first. In looking at the sketch for this chart, note that Andrea wants to group the data by states; that is, the four models are shown for each of the three states. The names of the states in cells B2:D2 of the worksheet will be used as category labels. The names of each stove model, in cells A3:A6, will represent the legend text. The data series for the chart are in rows B3:D3, B4:D4, B5:D5, and B6:D6.

Creating a Column Chart

After studying Andrea's sketch for the column chart, you are ready to create it, using the Sales Data worksheet. When you create a chart, you first select the cells that contain the data you want to appear in the chart and then you click the Chart Wizard button on the Standard toolbar. The Chart Wizard consists of four dialog boxes that guide you through the steps required to create a chart. Figure 4-6 identifies the tasks you perform in each of the Chart Wizard dialog boxes.

Figure 4-6 ◀
Tasks
performed in
each step of
the Chart
Wizard

Dialog Box	Tasks Performed
Chart Type	Select the type of chart you want to create—displays a list of chart types available in Excel; for each chart type, presents you with several chart subtypes from which you can choose
Chart Source Data	Specify the worksheet cells that contain the data and labels that will appear in the chart
Chart Options	Change the look of the chart by changing options that affect the titles, axes, gridlines, legends, data labels, and data tables
Chart Location	Specify where to place the chart: embedded in a work-sheet along with the worksheet data, or in a separate sheet called a chart sheet

You know that Andrea intends to create a handout of the worksheet and chart, so you want to embed the column chart in the same worksheet as the sales data, making it easier for her to create a one-page handout.

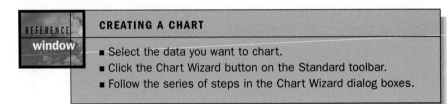

REFERENCE
window

CREATING A CHART

■ Select the data you want to chart.
■ Click the Chart Wizard button on the Standard toolbar.
■ Follow the series of steps in the Chart Wizard dialog boxes.

Before activating the Chart Wizard you will need to select the cells containing the data the chart will display. If you want the column and row labels to appear in the chart, include the cells that contain them in your selection as well. For this chart, select the range A2 through D6, which includes the sales of each Windsor stove model in the three states as well as names of the stove models and states.

To create the column chart using the Chart Wizard:

1. Select cells **A2:D6**, making sure no cells are highlighted in column E or row 7.

   Now that you have selected the chart range, you use the Chart Wizard to create the column chart.

2. Click the **Chart Wizard** button 📊 on the Standard toolbar to display the Chart Wizard - Step 1 of 4 - Chart Type dialog box. See Figure 4-7.

   TROUBLE? If the Office Assistant appears on your screen, click the button next to the message "No, don't provide help now" to close the Office Assistant.

   This first dialog box asks you to select the type of chart you want to create. The Chart type list box displays each of the 14 chart types available in Excel. The default chart type is the Column chart type. To the right of the Chart type list box is a gallery of chart subtypes for the selected chart. Select the chart type you want to create.

Figure 4-7 ◀
Chart Wizard -
Step 1 of 4 -
Chart Type
dialog box

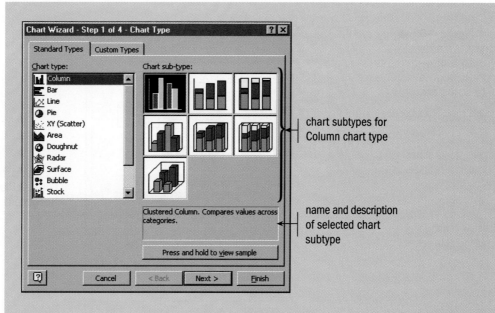

You want to create a column chart.

3. If necessary, click the **Column** chart type (the default) to select it. Seven Column chart subtypes are displayed. The Clustered Column chart subtype is the default subtype for the Column chart type. Click and hold the **Press and hold to view sample** button to display a preview of the Clustered Column chart subtype. See Figure 4-8. Release the mouse button.

To view any other Column chart subtype, select another subtype option and click the Press and hold to view sample button.

Figure 4-8 ◀
Preview of
Clustered
Column chart
type

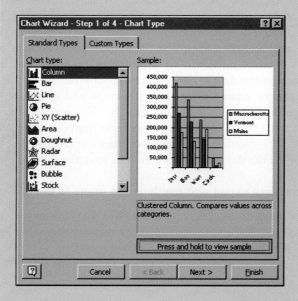

You decide to use the Clustered Column chart type, the default selection.

4. Click the **Next** button to display the Chart Wizard - Step 2 of 4 - Chart Source Data dialog box. See Figure 4-9. In this step you confirm or specify the worksheet cells that contain the data and labels to appear in the chart.

Figure 4-9 ◀
Chart Wizard -
Step 2 of 4 -
Chart Source
Data dialog box

current appearance
of chart

Andrea wants states
as category labels

Excel treating
columns in worksheet
as the data series

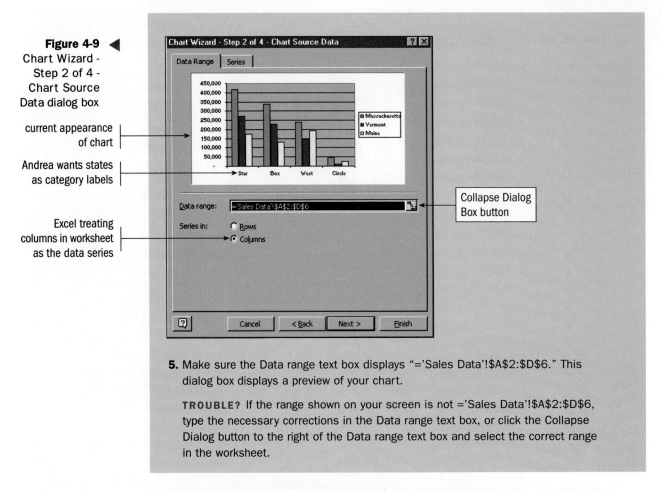

Collapse Dialog
Box button

5. Make sure the Data range text box displays "='Sales Data'!$A$2:$D$6." This
dialog box displays a preview of your chart.

TROUBLE? If the range shown on your screen is not ='Sales Data'!$A$2:$D$6,
type the necessary corrections in the Data range text box, or click the Collapse
Dialog button to the right of the Data range text box and select the correct range
in the worksheet.

In Step 2, you can also modify how the data series is organized—by rows or by
columns—using the **Series in** option. In Figure 4-9, the chart uses the columns in the
worksheet as the data series. To see how the chart would look if the rows in the worksheet were used as the data series, you can modify the settings in this dialog box.

Does the sample chart shown on your screen and in Figure 4-9 look like the sketch
Andrea prepared (Figure 4-5)? Not exactly. The problem is that the Chart Wizard
assumes that if the range to plot has more rows than columns (which is true in this case),
then the data in the columns (states) becomes the data series. Andrea wants the stove
models (rows) as the data series, so you need to make this change in the dialog box.

To change the data series and continue the steps in the Chart Wizard:

1. Click the **Rows** option button in the Series in area of the dialog box. The sample
chart now shows the stove models as the data series and the states as category
labels. See Figure 4-10.

Figure 4-10 ◀
Rows as data
series

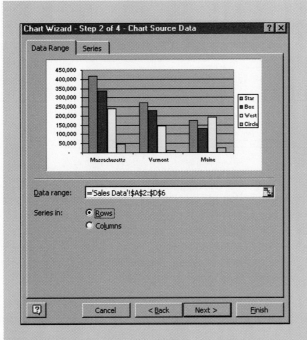

2. Click the **Next** button to display the Chart Wizard - Step 3 of 4 - Chart Options dialog box. See Figure 4-11. A preview area displays the current appearance of the chart. This tabbed dialog box enables you to change various chart options, such as titles, axes, gridlines, legends, data labels, and data tables. As you change these settings, check the preview chart in this dialog box to make sure you get the look you want.

   Now add a title for the chart.

Figure 4-11 ◀
Chart Wizard -
Step 3 of 4 -
Chart Options
dialog box

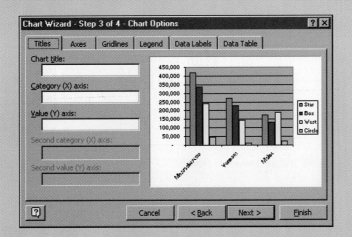

3. If necessary click the **Titles** tab, click the **Chart title** text box, and then type **Sales by State** for the chart title. Notice that the title appears in the preview area.

4. Click the **Next** button to display the Chart Wizard - Step 4 of 4 - Chart Location dialog box. See Figure 4-12. In this fourth dialog box you decide where to place the chart. You can place a chart in a worksheet, an embedded chart, or place it in its own chart sheet. You want to embed this chart in the Sales Data worksheet, which is the default option.

Figure 4-12 ◄
Chart Wizard -
Step 4 of 4 -
Chart Location
dialog box

You have finished the steps in the Chart Wizard.

5. Click the **Finish** button to complete the chart and display it in the Sales Data worksheet. See Figure 4-13. Notice the selection handles around the chart; these handles indicate that the chart is selected. The Chart toolbar is automatically displayed when the chart is selected. Also, notice that the data and labels for the chart are outlined in blue, green, and purple in the worksheet. This enables you to quickly see which cells make up the chart.

> **TROUBLE?** If you don't see the Chart toolbar, click View on the menu bar, click Toolbars, and then click the Chart check box to select that option.

Figure 4-13 ◄
Completed
column chart

indicates selected
chart element; click
list arrow to select
different element

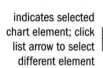

Chart Type button;
click list arrow to
select chart type

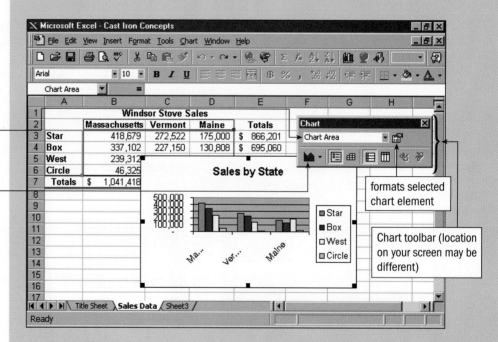

6. Click anywhere outside the chart to deselect it. Notice that the selection handles no longer surround the chart, indicating that the chart is no longer selected, and the Chart toolbar is no longer displayed. The Chart toolbar only appears when the chart is selected.

After reviewing the column chart, you think that the area outlined for the chart is too small to highlight the comparison between models. You also note that you need to move the chart so that it does not cover the worksheet data.

Moving and Resizing a Chart

When you use the Chart Wizard to create an embedded chart, Excel displays the chart in the worksheet. The size of the chart may not be large enough to accentuate relationships between data points or display the labels correctly. Since a chart is an object, you can move, resize, or copy it like any object in the Windows environment. However, before you can move, resize, or copy a chart, you must select, or **activate** it. You select a chart by clicking anywhere within the chart area. Small black squares, called **selection handles** or **sizing handles**, appear on the boundaries of the chart, indicating that it is selected. You will also notice that some of the items on the menu bar change to enable you to modify the chart instead of the worksheet.

You decide to move and resize the chart before showing it to Andrea.

To change the size and position of the chart:

1. Scroll the worksheet until row 8 appears as the first row in the window.

2. Click anywhere within the white area of the chart border to select the chart. Selection handles appear on the chart border. See Figure 4-14.

Figure 4-14 ◀
Selected chart

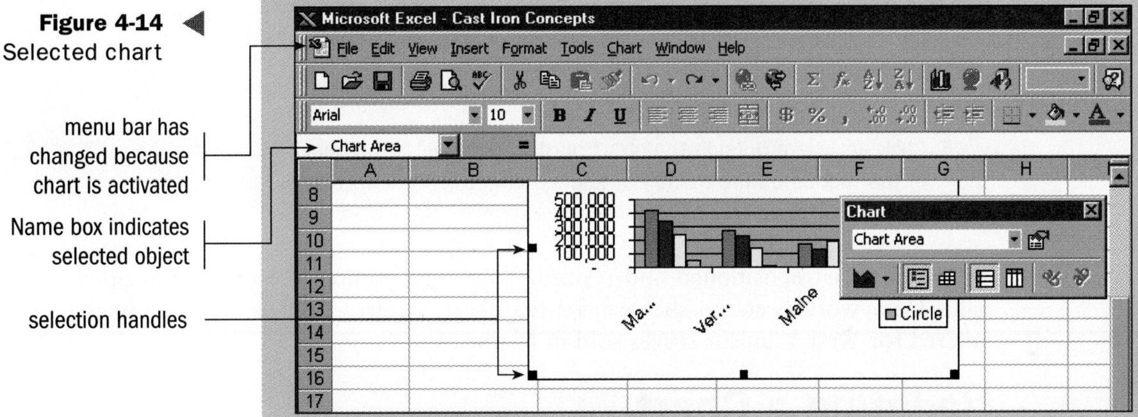

menu bar has
changed because
chart is activated

Name box indicates
selected object

selection handles

TROUBLE? If the Name box does not display the name "Chart Area," click the Chart Objects list box arrow on the Chart toolbar to display the list of chart objects. Select Chart Area.

TROUBLE? If the Chart toolbar is in the way, click and drag it to the bottom of the window to anchor it there.

3. Position the pointer anywhere on the chart border. The pointer changes to ⬚. Click and hold down the mouse button as you drag the chart down and to the left until you see the upper-left corner of the dashed outline in column A of row 8. Release the mouse button to view the chart in its new position.

Now increase the width of the chart.

4. Position the pointer on the right center selection handle. When the pointer changes to ↔, hold down the mouse button and drag the selection handle to the right until the chart outline reaches the right edge of column G. Release the mouse button to view the resized chart. See Figure 4-15.

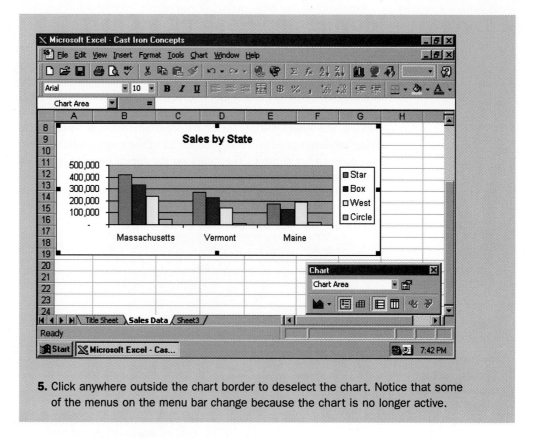

Figure 4-15 ◀
Chart after
being moved
and resized

5. Click anywhere outside the chart border to deselect the chart. Notice that some
of the menus on the menu bar change because the chart is no longer active.

The chart is repositioned and resized. You show Andrea the chart embedded in her
Sales Data worksheet. As she reviews the chart, Andrea notices an error in the value
entered for West Windsor stoves sold in Maine.

Updating a Chart

Every chart you create is linked to the worksheet data. As a result, if you change the data
in a worksheet, Excel automatically updates the chart to reflect the new values. Andrea
noticed that sales of West Windsor in Maine were entered incorrectly. She accidentally
entered sales as 191,500, when the correct entry should have been 119,500. Correct this
data entry error and observe how it changes the column chart.

To change the worksheet data and observe changes to the column chart:

1. Observe the height of the data marker for the West model in Maine (yellow data
marker) in the column chart.

2. Scroll the worksheet until row 2 appears as the first row of the worksheet window.

3. Click cell **D5**, and then type **119500** and press the **Enter** key. See Figure 4-16. The
total West sales (cell E5) and total sales for Maine (cell D7) automatically change.
In addition, Excel automatically updates the chart to reflect the new source value.
Now the data marker for the West Windsor sales in Maine is shorter.

Excel

Figure 4-16
Modified
column chart
after chart's
source data
changed

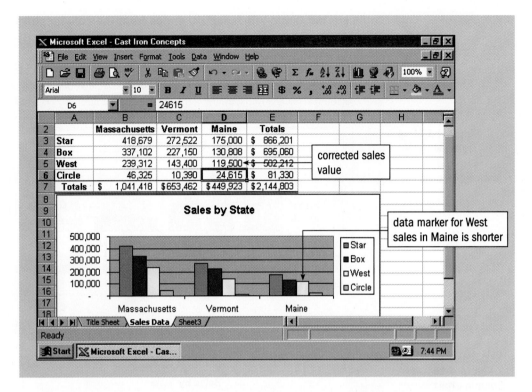

Now that the data for the West stove sales in Maine is corrected, you review the chart with Andrea for ways you can improve the presentation of the chart data.

Modifying an Excel Chart

You can make many modifications to a chart, including changing the type of chart, the text, the labels, the gridlines, and the titles. To make these modifications, you need to activate the chart. Selecting, or activating, a chart, as mentioned earlier, allows you to move and resize it. It also gives you access to the Chart commands on the menu bar and displays the Chart toolbar to use as you alter the chart.

After reviewing the column chart, Andrea believes that the Circle Windsor will distract the audience from the three products that were actually available during the entire period. Recall that the Circle Windsor was only on the market for four months and even then there were production problems. She wants to compare sales only for the three models sold during the entire year.

Revising the Chart Data Series

After you create a chart, you might discover that you specified the wrong data range, or you might decide that your chart should display different data series. Whatever your reason, you do not need to start over in order to revise the chart's data series.

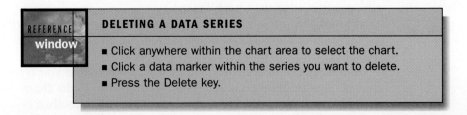

REFERENCE window

DELETING A DATA SERIES

- Click anywhere within the chart area to select the chart.
- Click a data marker within the series you want to delete.
- Press the Delete key.

Andrea asks you to remove the data series representing the Circle Windsor model from the column chart.

To delete the Circle Windsor data series from the column chart:

1. Click anywhere within the chart border to select the chart.

2. Click any data marker representing the Circle data series (any light blue data marker). Selection handles appear on each column of the Circle Windsor data series and a ScreenTip is displayed identifying the selected chart item. See Figure 4-17.

Figure 4-17 ◄
Chart with
Circle data
series selected

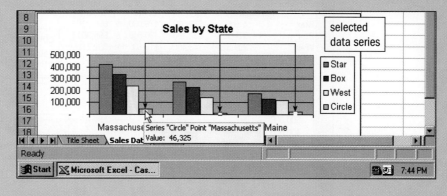

3. Press the **Delete** key. See Figure 4-18. Notice that the Circle Windsor data series is removed from the chart.

Figure 4-18 ◄
Column chart
after data
series removed

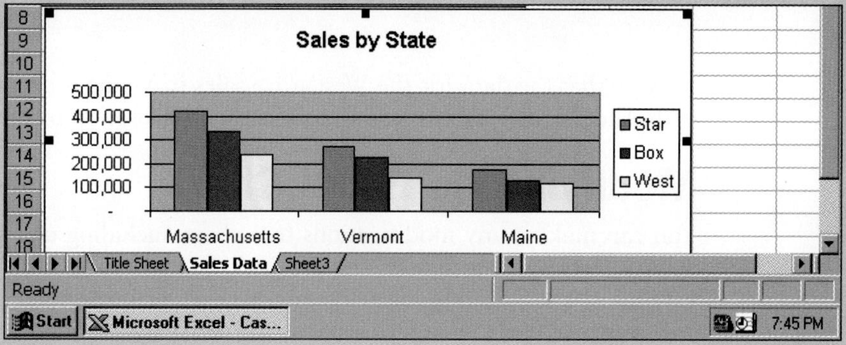

TROUBLE? If you deleted the wrong data series, click the Undo button 🔄 and repeat Steps 2 and 3.

Andrea reviews her sketch and notices that the chart title is incomplete; the intended title was "Sales by State and Model." She asks you to make this change to the chart.

Editing Chart Text

Excel classifies the text in your charts in three categories: label text, attached text, and unattached text. **Label text** includes the category names, the tick mark labels, the X-axis labels, and the legend. Label text often derives from the cells in the worksheet; you usually specify it using the Chart Wizard.

Attached text includes the chart title, X-axis title, and Y-axis title. Although attached text appears in a predefined position, you can edit it, and move it using the click-drag technique.

Unattached text includes text boxes or comments that you type in the chart after it is created. You can position unattached text anywhere in the chart. To add unattached text to a chart, you use the Text Box tool on the Drawing toolbar.

As noted earlier, you need to change the chart title to "Sales by State and Model." To do this you must select the chart, select the chart title, and then add "and Model" to the title.

To revise the chart title:

1. If the chart is not selected, click the **chart** to select it.

2. Click the **chart title** object to select it. Notice that the object name Chart Title appears in the Name box and as a ScreenTip; also, selection handles surround the Chart Title object.

3. Position the pointer in the chart title text box at the end of the title and click to remove the selection handles from the Chart Title object. The pointer changes to an insertion point I.

TROUBLE? If the insertion point is not at the end of the title, press the End key to move it to the end.

4. Press the **spacebar** and type **and Model**, and then click anywhere within the chart border to complete the change in the title and deselect it.

Checking Andrea's sketch, you notice that the Y-axis title was not included. To help clarify what the data values in the chart represent, you decide to add "Sales ($U.S.)" as a Y-axis title. You use the Chart Option command on the Chart menu to add this title.

To add the Y-axis title:

1. Make sure that the chart is still selected.

2. Click **Chart** on the menu bar, and then click **Chart Options** to display the Chart Options dialog box. If necessary, click the **Titles** tab.

3. Click the **Value (Y) axis** text box, and then type **Sales ($U.S.)**.

4. Click the **OK** button to close the Chart Options dialog box.

5. If necessary, scroll the worksheet so that the entire chart is displayed.

6. Click anywhere within the chart border to deselect the Y-axis title. See Figure 4-19.

Figure 4-19 ◄
Chart after title
modified and
value axis label
inserted

Value axis title ⎯⎯⎯⎯⎯

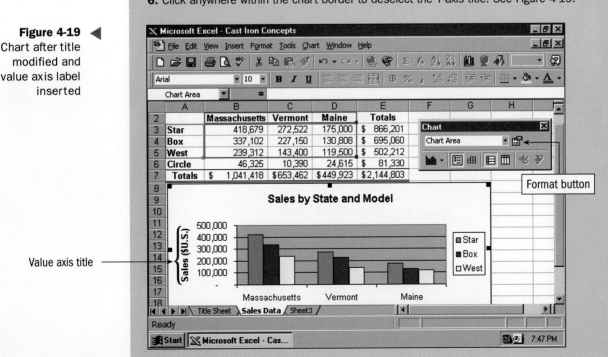

Now that the titles accurately describe the chart data, Andrea asks you to add data labels to show the exact values of the Star Windsor data series—CIC's leading model.

Adding Data Labels

A **data label** provides additional information about a data marker. Depending on the type of chart, data labels can show values, names of data series (or categories), or percentages. You can apply a label to a single data point, an entire data series, or all data markers in a chart.

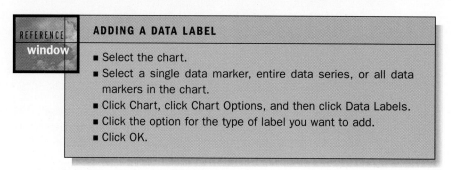

REFERENCE window	**ADDING A DATA LABEL**
	■ Select the chart.
	■ Select a single data marker, entire data series, or all data markers in the chart.
	■ Click Chart, click Chart Options, and then click Data Labels.
	■ Click the option for the type of label you want to add.
	■ Click OK.

In this case, Andrea wants to add data labels to the Star model data series.

To apply data labels to a data series:

1. If the column chart is not selected, click anywhere within the chart border to select it.

2. Click any **Star Windsor data marker** (blue data marker) within the chart. Selection handles appear on all columns in the Star Windsor data series.

   To format any chart element, you can use the Format button on the Chart toolbar. The Format button's ToolTip name and function change depending on what chart element is selected for formatting. The list box that appears to the left of the Format button on the toolbar also displays the name of the currently selected chart element. In this case, the Star Windsor data series marker is selected, so the Format button on the Chart toolbar appears as the Format Data Series button, and when selected, opens the Format Data Series dialog box.

3. Click the **Format Data Series** button 🖳 on the Chart toolbar to display the Format Data Series dialog box. Click the **Data Labels** tab if necessary. See Figure 4-20.

Figure 4-20 ◀
Active Data Labels tab in Format Data Series dialog box

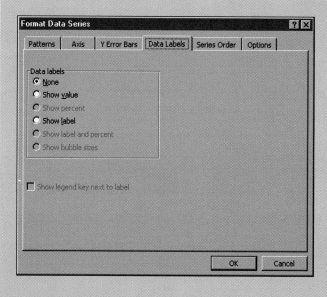

4. Click the **Show value** option button.

5. Click the **OK** button to display the column chart with data labels. See Figure 4-21.

Figure 4-21 ◀
Chart with data
labels

data labels ————

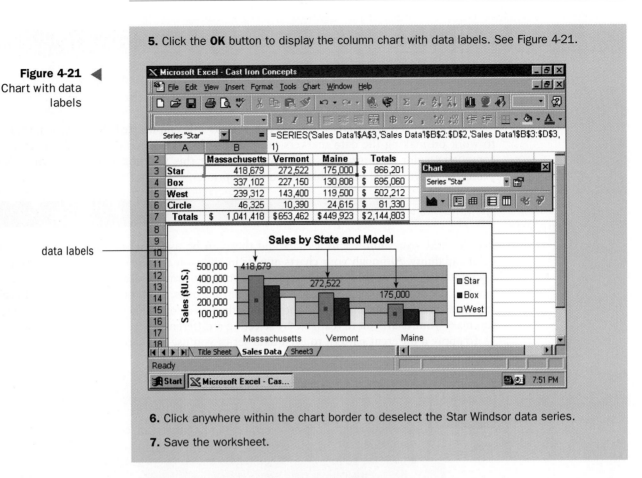

6. Click anywhere within the chart border to deselect the Star Windsor data series.

7. Save the worksheet.

Andrea is pleased with the changes in the chart's appearance. Now, she wants to add visual interest to the chart, making it look more polished.

Enhancing the Chart's Appearance

There are many ways to give charts a more professional look. The use of different font styles, types, and sizes can make chart labels and titles stand out. Also, using colors, borders, and patterns can make a chart more interesting to view.

Andrea thinks that a border and some color could accentuate the title of the chart.

Emphasizing the Title with Border and Color

The chart title is an object that you can select and format using the menu options or the toolbar buttons. Now make the changes to the chart title.

To display the title with border and color:

1. Click the **chart title** to select it and display selection handles. Now that the chart title is selected, notice that the Format button 🔲 on the Chart toolbar becomes the Format Chart Title button, and the Format button list box displays "Chart Title."

2. Click the **Format Chart Title** button 🔲 on the Chart toolbar to display the Format Chart Title dialog box, and then, if necessary, click the **Patterns** tab.

3. Click the **Weight** list arrow in the Border section to display a list of border weights.

4. Click the **second line** in the list.

5. Click the **gray** square in the Color palette (fourth row, last column) in the Area section.

6. Click the **OK** button to apply the format changes to the chart title, and then click anywhere within the chart area to deselect the title.

Andrea thinks that the chart looks better with its title emphasized. Now she wants you to work on making the data markers more distinctive. They certainly stand out on her computer's color monitor, but she is concerned that this will not be the case when she prints the chart on the office's black and white printer.

Changing Colors and Patterns

Patterns add visual interest to a chart and they can be useful when your printer has no color capability. Although your charts appear in color on a color monitor, if your printer does not have color capability, Excel translates colors to gray shades when printing. It's difficult to distinguish some colors, particularly darker ones, from one another when Excel translates them to gray shades and then prints them. To solve this potential problem, you can make your charts more readable by selecting a different pattern for each data marker.

To apply a different pattern to each data series you use the Patterns dialog box.

REFERENCE window	**SELECTING A PATTERN FOR A DATA MARKER**
	■ Make sure the chart is selected.
	■ Select the data marker or markers to which you want to apply a pattern.
	■ Click the Format Data Series button on the Chart toolbar to display the Format Data Series dialog box.
	■ Click the Patterns tab, click the Fill Effects button, and then click the Pattern tab to display a list of patterns.
	■ Click the pattern you want to apply, and then click the OK button twice to close the dialog boxes.

You want to apply a different pattern to each data series.

To apply a pattern to a data series:

1. Make sure the chart is selected.

2. Click any data marker for the Star data series (blue data marker) to display selection handles for all three data markers for that data series.

3. Click the **Format Data Series** button 🖻 on the Chart toolbar to display the Format Data Series dialog box.

4. If necessary, click the **Patterns** tab, and then click the **Fill Effects** button to display the Fill Effects dialog box. Click the **Pattern** tab to display the Pattern palette. See Figure 4-22.

Excel

Figure 4-22 ◀
Pattern options
in Fill Effects
dialog box

dark downward
diagonal pattern

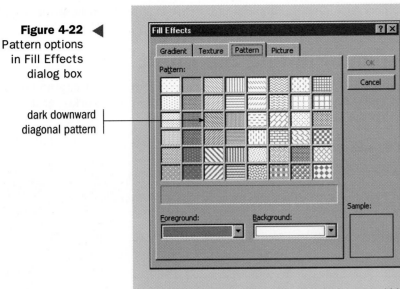

5. Click the **dark downward diagonal** pattern (third row, third column) to select it. Notice that the pattern you selected appears in the Sample box for you to preview.

6. Click the **OK** button to close the Fill Effects dialog box, and then click the **OK** button to close the Format Data Series dialog box and apply the pattern to the Star data series in the chart.

7. Repeat Steps 2 through 6 to select a narrow horizontal pattern (fourth row, fourth column) for the Box data series, and again to select a dark upward diagonal pattern (fourth row, third column) for the West data series. After you select patterns for the data series, your chart should look like Figure 4-23.

Figure 4-23 ◀
Patterned
column chart
data markers

pattern applied to
data marker

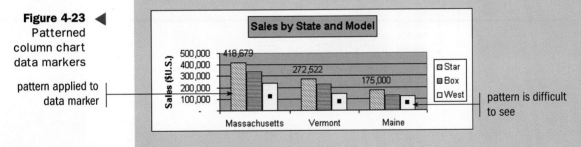

pattern is difficult
to see

You notice that the West markers appear to have no pattern applied because the pattern is very difficult to see when applied against the yellow color. You decide to change the color of the West markers to a darker color—green, so the pattern will be more visible.

To change the color of data markers:

1. If the West data markers are not selected, click any one of them to select the data markers for that data series.

2. Click the **Format Data Series** button 🖻 on the Chart toolbar to display the Format Data Series dialog box.

3. If necessary, click the **Patterns** tab, click the **Fill Effects** button, and then click the **Pattern** tab in the Fill Effects dialog box to display the patterns palette.

4. In the Pattern tab, click the **Background** list arrow to display a color palette. Click the **green** square in the third row, third column, and click the **OK** button to close the Fill Effects dialog box and return to the Format Data Series dialog box.

5. Click the **OK** button to close the Format Data Series dialog box, and then click anywhere outside the chart border to deselect the chart.

You show the chart to Andrea, and she decides that it is ready to be printed and duplicated for distribution at the meeting.

Previewing and Printing the Chart

Before you print you should preview the worksheet to see how it will appear on the printed page. Remember, Andrea wants the embedded chart and the worksheet data to print on one page that she can use as a handout at the meeting.

To save and print an embedded chart:

1. Click the **Save** button 🖫 on the Standard toolbar to save the workbook.

2. Click the **Print Preview** button 🔍 on the Standard toolbar to display the Print Preview window.

3. Click the **Print** button to display the Print dialog box, and then click the **OK** button. See Figure 4-24.

Figure 4-24 ◀
Printout of worksheet with embedded column chart

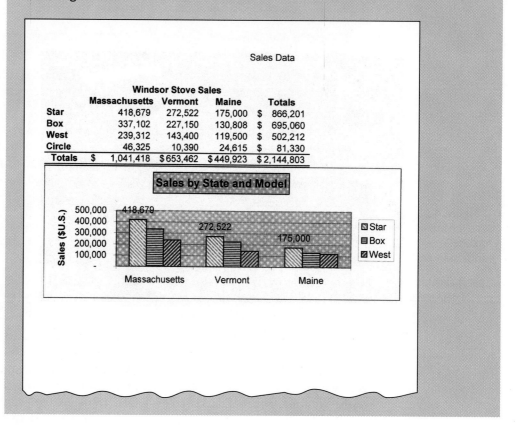

Quick Check

1. A column chart is used to show _____.

2. When you click an embedded chart, it is _____

3. Explain how to revise a chart's data series.

4. How do you move an embedded chart to a new location using the mouse?

5. Describe the action you're likely to take before beginning Step 1 of the Chart Wizard.

6. What happens when you change a value in a worksheet that is the source of data for a chart?

7 What is the purpose of a legend?

8 Explain the difference between a data point and a data marker.

You have finished creating the column chart showing stove sales by state and model for Andrea. Next, you need to create the pie chart showing total stove sales by model. You will do this in Session 4.2.

SESSION 4.2 *In this session you will create a pie chart. You will also learn how to select nonadjacent ranges, how to change a 2-D pie chart to a 3-D pie chart, and how to "explode" a slice from a pie chart. You will also learn how to use chart sheets and how to add a border to a chart.*

Creating a Chart in a Chart Sheet

Now Andrea wants to show the contribution of each Windsor model to the total stove sales. Recall from the planning sketch she did (Figure 4-5) that she wants to use a pie chart to show this relationship.

A pie chart shows the relationship, or proportions, of parts to a whole. The size of each slice is determined by the value of that data point in relation to the total of all values. A pie chart contains only one data series. When you create a pie chart, you generally specify two ranges. Excel uses the first range for the category labels and the second range for the data series. Excel automatically calculates the percentage for each slice, draws the slice to reflect the percentage of the whole, and gives you the option of displaying the percentage as a label in the completed chart.

Andrea's sketch (see Figure 4-5) shows estimates of each stove's contribution and how she wants the pie chart to look. The pie chart will have four slices, one for each stove model. She wants each slice labeled with the stove model's name and its percentage of total sales. Because she doesn't know the exact percentages until Excel calculates and displays them in the chart, she put "__%" on her sketch to show where she wants the percentages to appear.

Creating a Pie Chart

You begin creating a pie chart by selecting the data to be represented from the worksheet. You refer to your worksheet and note in the sketch that the data labels for the pie slices are in cells A3 through A6 and the data points representing the pie slices are in cells E3 through E6. You must select these two ranges to tell the Chart Wizard the data that you want to chart, but you realize that these ranges are not located next to each other in the worksheet. You know how to select a series of adjacent cells; now you need to learn how to select two separate ranges at once.

Selecting Nonadjacent Ranges

A **nonadjacent range** is a group of individual cells or ranges that are not next to each other. Selecting nonadjacent ranges is particularly useful when you construct charts because the cells that contain the data series and these that contain the data labels are often not side by side in the worksheet. When you select nonadjacent ranges, the selected cells in each range are highlighted. You can then format the cells, clear them, or use them to construct a chart.

SELECTING NONADJACENT RANGES

- Click the first cell or highlight the first range you want to select.
- Press and hold the Ctrl key while you click additional cells or highlight additional ranges.
- After you select all the cells you want to include, release the Ctrl key.

Now select the nonadjacent ranges to be used to create the pie chart.

To select range A3:A6 and range E3:E6 in the Sales Data sheet:

1. If you took a break after the last session, make sure that Excel is running, the Cast Iron Concepts workbook is open, and the Sales Data worksheet is displayed.

2. Click anywhere outside the chart border to make sure the chart is not activated. Press **Ctrl + Home** to make cell A1 the active cell.

3. Select cells **A3** through **A6**, and then release the mouse button.

4. Press and hold the **Ctrl** key while you select cells **E3** through **E6**, and then release the mouse and the Ctrl key. The two nonadjacent ranges are now selected: A3:A6 and E3:E6. See Figure 4-25.

   TROUBLE? If you don't select the cells you want on your first try, click any cell to remove the highlighting, then go back to Step 2 and try again.

Figure 4-25
Selecting nonadjacent cell ranges

nonadjacent ranges selected

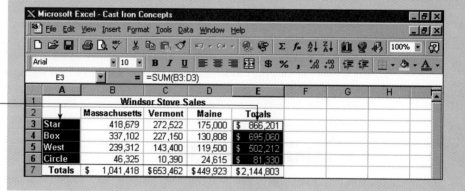

This time you'll place your new chart in a **chart sheet,** a special sheet that contains only one chart. It does not have the rows and columns of a regular worksheet. If you have many charts to create, you may want to place each chart in a separate chart sheet to avoid cluttering the worksheet. This approach also makes it easier to locate a particular chart because you can change the name on the chart sheet tab.

To create a pie chart in a chart sheet:

1. Click the **Chart Wizard** button on the Standard toolbar to display the Chart Wizard - Step 1 of 4 - Chart Type dialog box.

   TROUBLE? If the Office Assistant appears on your screen, click the button next to the message "No, don't provide help now" to close the Office Assistant.

   You want to create a pie chart.

2. Click the **Pie** chart type to select it. Six Pie chart subtypes are displayed. The Two-dimensional Pie chart subtype is the default subtype for the Pie chart type. Click the **Press and hold to view sample** button to display a preview of the Pie chart type.

You decide to use the default chart subtype.

3. Click the **Next** button to display the Chart Wizard - Step 2 of 4 - Chart Source Data dialog box. Make sure the Data range text box displays "='Sales Data'!$A$3:$A$6,'Sales Data'!$E$3:$E$6." This dialog box also displays a preview of your chart.

   TROUBLE? If the range shown on your screen is not "='Sales Data'!$A$3:$A$6, 'Sales Data'!$E$3:$E$6," type the necessary corrections in the Data range text box, or click the Collapse Dialog button located to the right of the Data range text box and select the correct range in the worksheet.

4. Click the **Next** button to display the Chart Wizard - Step 3 of 4 - Chart Options dialog box.

   Add a title for the chart.

5. If necessary, click the **Titles** tab, click the **Chart title** text box, and then type **Sales by Model** for the chart title. Notice that the title appears in the preview area.

6. Click the **Data Labels** tab, and then click the **Show label and percent** option button to place the label and percent next to each slice.

   Now remove the legend because it is no longer needed.

7. Click the **Legend** tab, and then click the **Show legend** check box to remove the check and deselect that option.

8. Click the **Next** button to display the Chart Wizard - Step 4 of 4 - Chart Location dialog box. Recall that in the fourth dialog box you decide where to place the chart. You can place a chart in a worksheet, or place it in its own chart sheet. You want to place this chart in a chart sheet.

9. Click the **As new sheet** option button to place the chart in the Chart1 chart sheet.

   You have finished the steps in the Chart Wizard.

10. Click the **Finish** button to complete the chart. The new chart, along with the Chart toolbar, appears in the chart sheet named Chart1. The chart sheet is inserted into the workbook before the worksheet on which it is based. If necessary, click the white portion of chart area to select the chart. See Figure 4-26.

Figure 4-26 ◀
Pie chart in a
chart sheet

default name for
first chart sheet

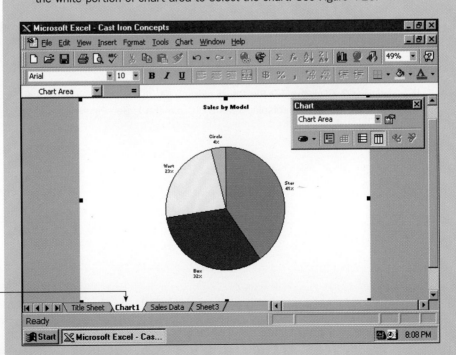

After reviewing the pie chart, Andrea asks you to change the current pie chart to a three-dimensional design to give the chart a more professional look.

Changing the Chart Type from 2-D to 3-D

As you recall, Excel provides 14 different chart types that you can choose from as you create a chart. You can also access these chart types after the chart is created and change from one type to another. To change the chart type, you can use the Chart Type command on the Chart menu or the Chart Type button on the Chart toolbar to make this change. You'll use the Chart toolbar to change this 2-D pie chart to a 3-D pie chart.

To change the pie chart to a 3-D pie chart:

1. Make sure the chart area is selected, and then click the **Chart Type** [icon] arrow on the Chart toolbar to display a palette of chart types. See Figure 4-27.

   TROUBLE? If the Chart toolbar is not displayed on the screen, click View on the menu bar, point to Toolbars, and click the Chart check box to display the Chart toolbar.

Figure 4-27 ◀
Palette of
chart types

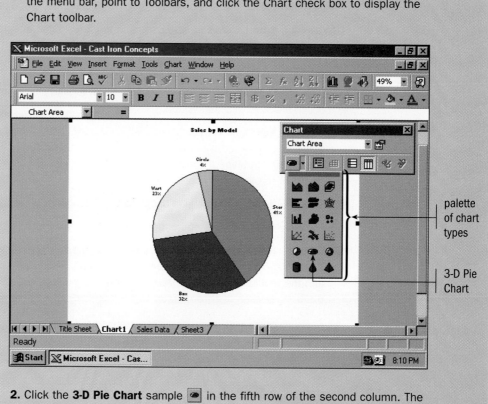

palette
of chart
types

3-D Pie
Chart

2. Click the **3-D Pie Chart** sample [icon] in the fifth row of the second column. The chart is redisplayed as a 3-D pie chart. See Figure 4-28.

Figure 4-28 ◀
3-D pie chart

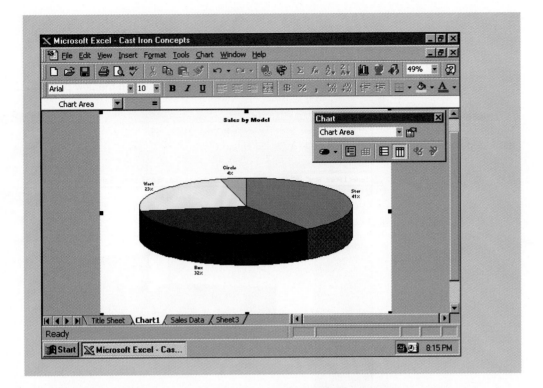

In her presentation, Andrea plans to emphasize the importance of the Star model because it is her best-selling model in the New England territory. She decides to "explode" the Star slice.

Exploding a Slice of a Pie Chart

When you create a pie chart, you may want to focus attention on a particular slice in the chart. You can present the data so a viewer can easily see which slice is larger or smaller—for example, which product sold the most. One method of emphasizing a particular slice over others is by separating the slice from the rest of the pie. The *cut* slice is more distinct because it is not connected to the other slices. A pie chart with one or more slices separated from the whole is referred to as an **exploded pie chart**.

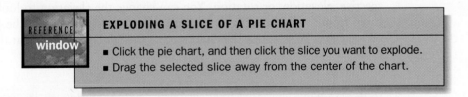

REFERENCE
window

EXPLODING A SLICE OF A PIE CHART

- Click the pie chart, and then click the slice you want to explode.
- Drag the selected slice away from the center of the chart.

Andrea asks you to explode the slice that represents sales for the Star model.

To explode the slice that represents the Star model sales:

1. Click anywhere in the pie chart to select it. One selection handle appears on each pie slice and the Name box indicates that Series 1 is the selected chart object.

2. Now that you have selected the entire pie, you can select one part of it, the Star slice. Position the pointer over the slice that represents Star model sales. As you move the pointer over this slice, the ScreenTip "Series 1 Point: "Star" Value: $866,201 (41%)" is displayed. Click to select the slice. Selection handles now appear on only this slice.

3. With the pointer on the selected slice, click and hold down the mouse button while dragging the slice to the right, away from the center of the pie chart. As you drag the slice, an outline of the slice marks your progress.

4. Release the mouse button to leave the slice in the new position. See Figure 4-29.

Figure 4-29 ◀
Pie chart with exploded slice

exploded slice

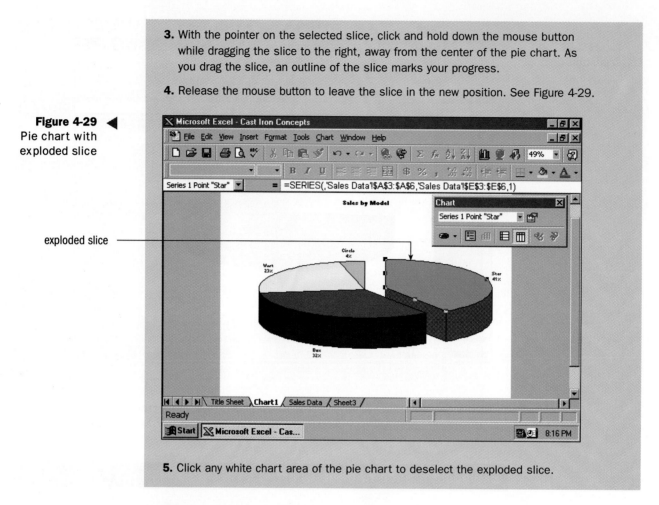

5. Click any white chart area of the pie chart to deselect the exploded slice.

The Star model now is exploded in the pie chart, but Andrea still isn't satisfied. You suggest moving the slice to the front of the pie.

Rotating a 3-D Chart

When working with a 3-D chart, you can modify the view of your chart to change its perspective, elevation, or rotation. You can change the elevation to look down on the chart or up from the bottom. You can also rotate the chart to adjust the placement of objects on the chart. Now rotate the chart so that the Star slice appears at the front of the chart.

To change the 3-D view of the chart:

1. Click **Chart** on the menu bar, and then click **3-D View** to display the 3-D View dialog box. See Figure 4-30.

Figure 4-30 ◀
3-D View dialog box

clockwise rotation arrow button

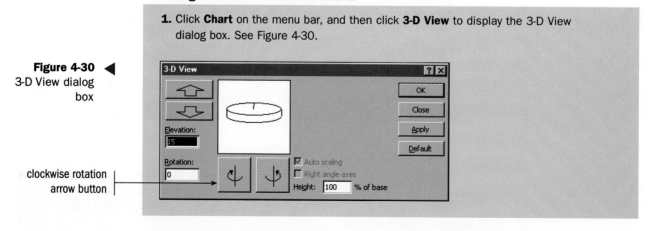

2. Click the **clockwise rotation arrow** button until the Rotation box shows 90; as you do this, notice that the pie chart sketch rotates to show the new position.

3. Click the **OK** button to apply the changes. See Figure 4-31.

Figure 4-31 ◀
3-D pie chart
after view
rotated to
display cut
slice in front

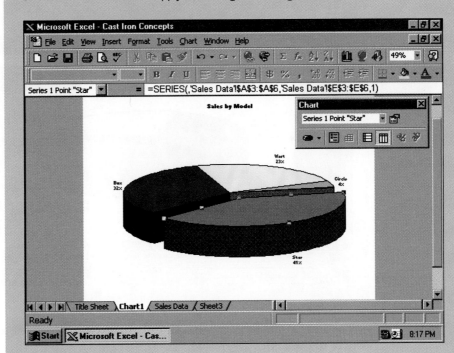

After looking over the chart, you decide to increase the size of the chart labels so that they are easier to read.

Formatting Chart Labels

You can change the font type, size, style, and the color of text in a chart using the Formatting toolbar buttons.

You look at the chart and decide that it will look better if you increase the size of the data labels from 10 to 14 points.

To change the font size of the chart labels:

1. Click any one of the four data labels to select all the data labels. Selection handles appear around all four labels, and the Name box displays "Series 1 Data Labels."

2. Click the **Font Size** list arrow on the Formatting toolbar, and then click **14**.

Now increase the font size of the title to 20 points.

To change the font size of the chart title:

1. Click the **chart title** to select it. Selection handles appear around the title.

2. Click the **Font Size** list arrow on the Formatting toolbar, and then click **20**.

3. Click any white area of the pie chart to deselect the title. See Figure 4-32.

Figure 4-32 ◄
3-D pie chart
after font size
of data labels
and title
increased

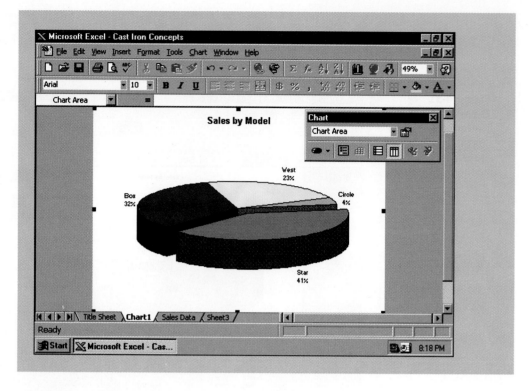

The pie chart looks good but Andrea has one last request. She asks you to apply a blue texture to the chart background.

Applying a Texture Fill Effect to the Chart Background

You can apply texture or gradient fill effects to chart walls, floors, bars, columns, and chart and plot background areas. These fill effects provide a professional look. You want to change the white chart area of the pie chart to a blue texture.

To apply a texture fill effect to the chart background:

1. Make sure the chart area is selected. If it is not, click the white area around the pie chart.

2. Click the **Format Chart Area** button 🖼 on the Chart toolbar to display the Format Chart Area dialog box.

3. If necessary, click the **Patterns** tab, click the **Fill Effects** button to display the Fill Effects dialog box, and then click the **Texture** tab. See Figure 4-33.

Figure 4-33 ◀
Texture options
in Fill Effects
dialog box

blue tissue
paper texture

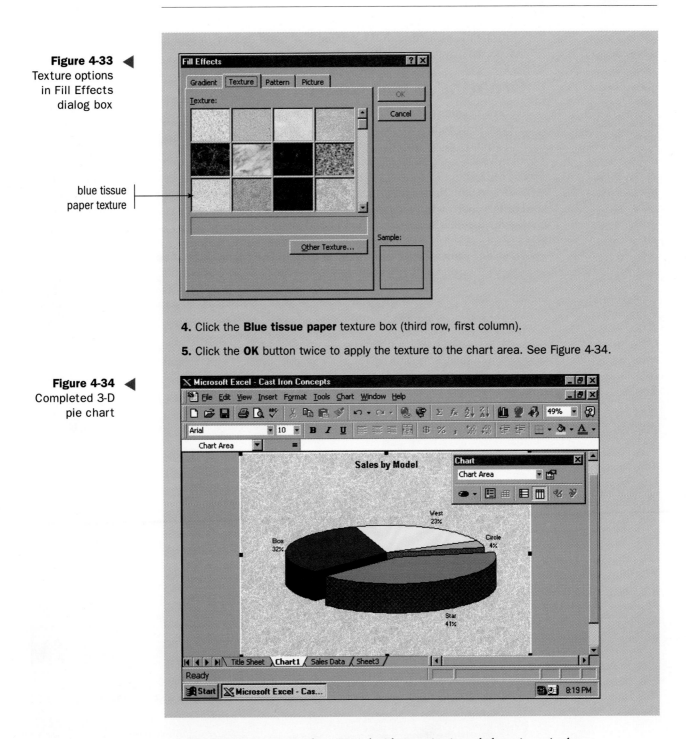

4. Click the **Blue tissue paper** texture box (third row, first column).

5. Click the **OK** button twice to apply the texture to the chart area. See Figure 4-34.

Figure 4-34 ◀
Completed 3-D
pie chart

The chart is now complete. You decide to print it and show it to Andrea.

Printing the Chart from the Chart Sheet

When you create a chart in a separate sheet, you can print that sheet separately. If necessary, you can make page setup decisions for the chart sheet alone. In this case, the chart in the chart sheet is ready for printing. You don't need to change any setup options. Now that the 3-D pie chart is complete, save the workbook and print a copy of the chart.

To save the workbook and print the chart:

1. Click the **Save** button 🖫 on the Standard toolbar to save the workbook.

2. Click the **Print** button 🖨 on the Standard toolbar to print the chart.

Andrea is pleased with the printed chart and believes it will help her when she makes her presentation next week.

Creating a Bar Chart

Andrea decides to spend some time during her presentation reviewing sales of all stoves in each state in her territory. She recalls from one of her college classes that both the bar and column chart are useful for comparing data by categories. The bar chart may have an advantage if you have long labels, because the category labels in bar charts are easier to read. Andrea asks you to prepare a bar chart comparing sales of all stoves by state.

To prepare this chart, you will first select the cells containing the chart you will display. For this chart, select the range B2 through D2 for the category axis (states) and B7 through D7 for the data series (total sales in each state).

To select range B2:D2 and range B7:D7 in the Sales Data sheet:

1. Click the **Sales Data** tab to activate the Sales Data worksheet, and then press **Ctrl + Home** to make cell A1 the active cell.

2. Select cells **B2:D2**, and then release the mouse button.

3. Press and hold the **Ctrl** key while you select cells **B7:D7**, and then release the mouse and the Ctrl key. The two nonadjacent ranges are now selected: B2:D2 and B7:D7.

   TROUBLE? If you don't select the cells you want on your first try, click any cell to remove the highlighting, and then go back to Step 2 and try again.

Place the bar chart in a separate chart sheet so that Andrea can easily locate it.

To create a bar chart in a chart sheet:

1. Click the **Chart Wizard** button 📊 on the Standard toolbar to display the Chart Wizard - Step 1 of 4 - Chart Type dialog box.

   You want to create a bar chart.

2. Click the **Bar** chart type to select it. Six Bar chart subtypes are displayed. The Clustered Bar chart is the default subtype for the Bar chart. Click the **Press and hold to view sample** button to display a preview of the Clustered Bar chart subtype.

   You decide to use the Clustered Bar chart type.

3. Click the **Next** button to display the Chart Wizard - Step 2 of 4 - Chart Source Data dialog box. Make sure the Data range box displays "='Sales data'!$B$2:$D$2,'Sales Data'!$B$7:$D$7." This dialog box also displays a preview of your chart.

   TROUBLE? If the range shown on your screen is not "='Sales data'!$B$2:$D$2, 'Sales Data'!$B$7:$D$7," type the necessary corrections in the Data range text box, or click the Collapse Dialog button and select the correct range in the worksheet.

4. Click the **Next** button to display the Chart Wizard - Step 3 of 4 - Chart Options dialog box.

   Add a title for the chart.

5. If necessary, click the **Titles** tab, and then click the **Chart title** text box. Type **Sales by State** for the chart title. Notice that the title appears in the preview area. Click the **Category (X) axis** title box, and then type **Territories**. Click the **Value (Y) axis** title box, and then type **Sales ($U.S.)**.

   Since there is only one data series, remove the legend.

6. Click the **Legend** tab and then click the **Show legend** check box to remove the check and deselect that option.

7. Click the **Next** button to display the Chart Wizard - Step 4 of 4 - Chart Location dialog box. You want this chart to be placed in a chart sheet.

8. Click the **As new sheet** option button to place this chart in a chart sheet, and then type **Bar Chart** in the As new sheet text box to rename the chart sheet.

You have finished the steps in the Chart Wizard.

9. Click the **Finish** button to complete the chart. The new chart, along with the Chart toolbar, appears in the chart sheet named Bar Chart. The chart sheet is inserted into the workbook before the worksheet on which it is based. See Figure 4-35.

Figure 4-35 ◄
Bar chart in a
chart sheet

categories are
organized vertically

values are displayed
horizontally

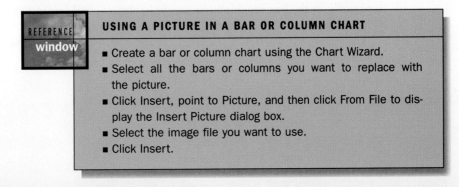

Andrea reviews the bar chart and believes it will focus the audience's attention on sales in each state.

Using Pictures in a Bar Chart

When making a presentation, an interesting way to enhance a bar or column chart is to replace the data markers with graphic images, thereby creating a picture chart. Any graphic image that can be copied to the Clipboard can serve as the basis for a picture chart. Andrea wants you to use a picture of the Windsor stove from CIC's latest catalog as the data marker in your bar chart.

REFERENCE window	**USING A PICTURE IN A BAR OR COLUMN CHART**
	■ Create a bar or column chart using the Chart Wizard.
	■ Select all the bars or columns you want to replace with the picture.
	■ Click Insert, point to Picture, and then click From File to display the Insert Picture dialog box.
	■ Select the image file you want to use.
	■ Click Insert.

The graphic image of the Windsor stove is located in the Tutorial.04 folder on your Student Disk. The file is named Stove. To replace the plain bars with the graphic image, you need to select one bar or column of the chart and use the Picture command on the Insert menu.

To insert the picture into the bar chart:

1. Click any column in the chart so that all three data markers are selected.

2. Click **Insert** on the menu bar, point to **Picture,** and then click **From File** to display the Insert Picture dialog box.

3. Make sure Tutorial.04 is the folder shown in the Look In list box, and then click **Stove**.

4. Click the **Insert** button to insert the picture into the chart. The three bars are each filled by the picture of the stove. See Figure 4-36. Notice that each picture is "stretched" to fit the bar it fills.

Figure 4-36 ◀
Picture chart
with stretched
graphic

Stove graphic ────

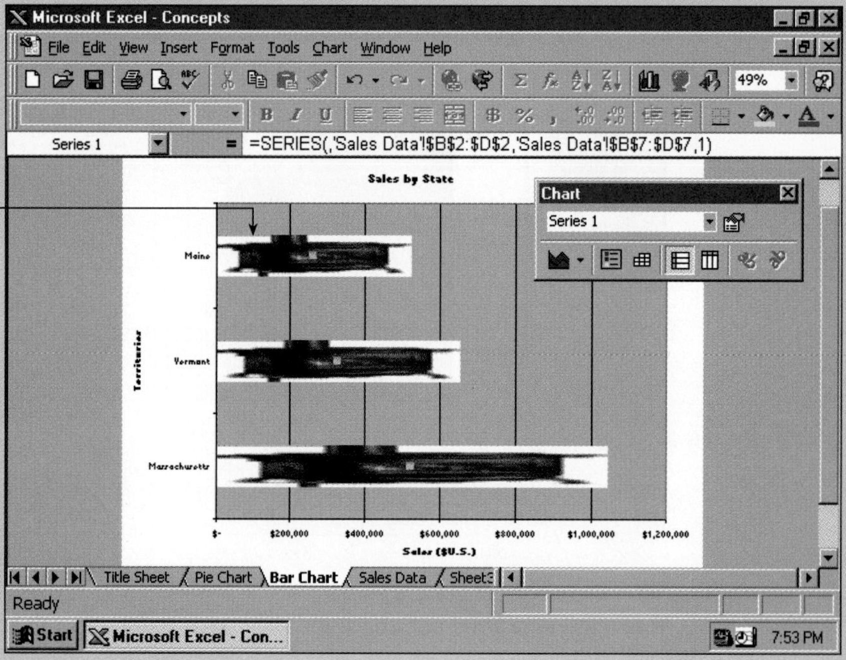

When you insert a picture into a bar or column chart, Excel automatically stretches the picture to fill the space formerly occupied by the marker. Some pictures stretch well, but others become distorted, and detract from, rather than add to, the chart's impact.

Stretching and Stacking Pictures

As an alternative to stretching a picture, you can stack the picture so that it appears repeatedly in the bar, reaching the height of the original bar in the chart. You'll stack the Windsor stove picture in your chart to improve its appearance.

The value axis has tick mark labels at 200000, 400000, 600000, and so on. To match the axis labels, you'll stack one stove each 200000 units.

To stack the picture:

1. If the handles have disappeared from the bars, click any bar in the chart to select all the bars.

2. Click the **Format Data Series** button 🖼 on the Chart toolbar to display the Format Data Series dialog box, and if necessary, click the **Patterns** tab.

3. Click the **Fill Effects** button to display the Fill Effects dialog box, and then click the **Picture** tab.

4. Click the **Stack and scale to** option button. Accept the Units/Picture value.

5. Click the **OK** button to close the Fill Effects dialog box, and then click the **OK** button to close the Format Data Series dialog box and return to the chart sheet and display the data markers as stacked stoves.

6. Click the white area of the chart to deselect the data markers. See Figure 4-37.

Figure 4-37 ◀
Picture chart
with stacked
graphic

stacked graphic
image

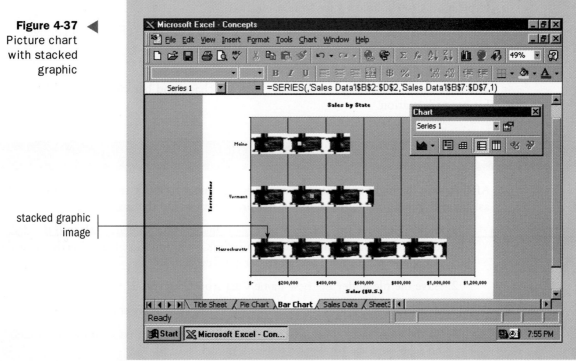

Andrea likes the picture chart, but is not sure how her audience will react to this type of chart. She wants to think about it. She asks you to save the workbook with the picture chart included and will let you know in the morning whether to print the picture chart or return to the bar chart. If Andrea asks you to remove the pictures and return to the original bars for the data markers, you will select the data series, click Edit, click Clear, and then click Formats.

Now save the workbook.

To save the workbook:

1. Click the **Title Sheet** tab to make it the active worksheet.

2. Click the **Save** button 🖫 on the Standard toolbar.

3. Close the workbook and exit Excel.

Quick Check

1 Define the following terms in relation to a pie chart:
   a. data point
   b. data marker
   c. data series

2 Explain how to select cells A1, C5, and D10 at the same time.

3 What type of chart shows the proportion of parts to a whole?

4 When creating charts, why is it important to know how to select nonadjacent ranges?

5 Explain the difference between an embedded chart and a chart placed in a chart sheet.

6 Explain how to rotate a 3-D pie chart.

7 Explain how to explode a slice from a pie chart.

8 When you change a two-dimensional pie chart to a 3-D pie chart, you change the _____.

You have finished creating the column chart, pie chart, and bar chart that Andrea needs for her presentation.

Tutorial Assignments

After having the night to think about it, Andrea comes to work the next morning and asks you to create one more chart for her presentation. Do the following:

1. Start Windows and Excel, if necessary. Insert your Student Disk into the disk drive. Make sure that the Excel and Book1 windows are maximized. Open the file Concept2 in the TAssign folder for Tutorial 4.

2. Save the file under the new name Cast Iron Concepts 2 in the TAssign folder.

3. Type your name and the current date in the Title Sheet sheet.

4. In the Sales Data sheet select the nonadjacent ranges that contain the models (A3:A6) and the total sales for each model (E3:E6).

5. Use the Chart Wizard to create a clustered column chart with 3-D visual effect. Place the completed chart in a chart sheet.

6. As you are creating the chart, remove the legend and add "Total Stove Sales by State" as the chart title.

7. Rename the chart sheet "3D Column."

8. After the chart is completed, increase the font size of the title and axis labels so that they are easier to read.

9. Put a box around the chart's title, using a thick line for a border. Add a drop shadow to the border.

10. Save the workbook. Print the chart. Include your name, the filename, and the date in the footer for the printed chart.

11. Select the walls chart element and apply a 1-color gradient fill effect. You select an appropriate color.

12. Select the value axis and change its scale so that the major unit is 150000.

Excel

 13. Open the Office Assistant and learn how you can show the worksheet data in a data table, which is a grid at the bottom of the chart. (*Hint:* Search on "add data table to a chart.") Add a data table to your chart. Increase the font size associated with the data table.

14. Save the workbook, and then print the chart.

 15. Switch to the Sales Data worksheet and do the following:

   a. Change the color of the West Windsor pattern to brown.

   b. Move the legend to the bottom of the chart. Increase the height of the chart, so it has a more professional look.

   c. Annotate the column chart with the note "Star model—best seller in Massachusetts!" by adding a text box and arrow using the tools on the Drawing toolbar.

   d. Save the workbook, and then print the Sales Data sheet with the embedded chart.

Case Problems

1. Illustrating Production Data at TekStar Electronics You are executive assistant to the President of TekStar Electronics, a manufacturer of consumer electronics. You are compiling the yearly manufacturing reports and have collected production totals for each of TekStar's four U.S. manufacturing plants. The workbook TekStar contains these totals. Now you need to create a 3-D pie chart showing the relative percentage of CD players each plant produced.

1. Open the workbook Tekstar in the Case folder for Tutorial 4 and add the necessary information to the Title Sheet sheet to create a summary of the workbook. Save the workbook as TekStar Electronics in the Case folder for Tutorial 4.

2. Activate the Units Sold sheet. Use the Chart Wizard to create a 3-D pie chart in a chart sheet that shows the percentage of CD players produced at each plant location. Use the Pie with 3-D Visual Effect subtype.

3. Enter "Production of CD Players" as the chart title. Show "Label" and "Percent" as the data labels. Remove the legend.

4. Pull out the slice representing the Chicago plant's CD player production.

5. Increase the font size of the title and data labels so that they are easier to read.

6. Name the chart sheet 3D Pie Chart.

7. Preview and print the chart sheet. Save your work.

8. Create an embedded chart comparing sales of all the products by city. Select the appropriate range and then use the Chart Wizard to create a clustered bar chart. Use the products as the data series and the cities as the X-axis (category) labels. Enter "Production by Product and Plant Location" as the title.

9. Move the bar chart under the table, and then enhance the chart in any way you think appropriate.

10. Preview and print the embedded bar chart. Save your work.

11. Create a clustered column chart with 3-D visual effect comparing the production of VCRs by city. Remove the legend. Place the chart in a chart sheet named "VCRs."

   a. Add a data table (a grid in a chart that contains the numeric data used to create the chart) to the chart. (*Hint*: Use the Office Assistant to find out how to add a data table to a chart.)
   b. Save the workbook, and then print the chart.

2. Dow Jones Charting You are working for a stock analyst who is planning to publish a weekly newsletter. One regular component of the newsletter will be a 15-week chart tracking the Dow Jones average. Create the chart that can be used for the newsletter.

   1. Open the workbook DowJones in the Case folder for Tutorial 4. Save the workbook as Dow Jones 8-2-96 in the Case folder for Tutorial 4.

   2. Use the Chart Wizard to create an embedded line chart (Line subtype) in the Data worksheet. Specify "Dow Jones Average" as the chart title and "Index" as the title for the Y-axis. Do not add a legend or X-axis title.

   3. Place the chart to the right of the present worksheet data and resize it until you are satisfied with its appearance.

   4. Edit the chart as follows:

      a. Change the line marker to a thick line.
      b. Apply a texture fill effect to the chart area. You decide the texture.
      c. Change the color of the plot area to a shade of yellow.
      d. Angle the text upward for the dates on the category axis.

   5. Save your workbook. Preview and print the embedded chart.

   6. Add the text box "Inflation Worries Wall Street" pointing to 7-26-96.

   7. Save your workbook. Print the chart.

   8. The Dow Jones average for the week ending 8-9-96 was 5500.

      a. Add this data to the last row of the worksheet.
      b. Modify the chart by plotting the 15-week period beginning 5-3-96 and ending 8-9-96.
      c. Save the workbook as Dow Jones 8-9-96. Preview your work and print only the chart. Center the chart vertically and horizontally on the page.

3. *New York Chronicle* You are working as an intern for Jeff Sindle, business economist, of the *New York Chronicle*—a New York newspaper with circulation in New York City and Long Island. The paper is planning to publish an economic profile of the region and you are assisting in this project.

   1. Open the workbook NewYork in the Case folder for Tutorial 4. Save the workbook as New York Economic Data. Create three charts, each in its own chart sheet.

   2. First, create a 3-D pie chart that compares the population of the six geographic areas in the study. Title the chart and enhance it as you think appropriate. Rename the chart sheet to reflect the chart it contains.

   3. Create a clustered column chart that compares the number of establishments in retail and services by the six geographic areas. (*Hint*: Categorize by type of establishment; each geographic area is a data series.) Title the chart and enhance it as you think appropriate. Rename the chart sheet to reflect the chart it contains.

4. Create a clustered bar chart comparing sales/receipts by geographic area (categorize by geographic area; the data series is sales/receipts). Title the chart and enhance it as you think appropriate. Rename the chart sheet to reflect the chart it contains.

5. Add a title sheet that includes your name, date created, purpose, and a brief description of each sheet in the workbook.

6. Save the workbook.

7. Print the entire workbook (title and data worksheet and the three chart sheets).

4. Duplicating a Printed Chart Look through books, business magazines, or textbooks for your other courses to find an attractive chart. Select one, photocopy it, and create a worksheet that contains the data displayed in the chart. You can estimate the data values plotted in the chart. Do your best to duplicate the chart you found. You might not be able to duplicate the chart fonts or colors exactly, but choose the closest available substitutes. When your work is complete, save it as Duplicate Chart in the Case folder for Tutorial 4, preview it, and print it. Submit the photocopy of the original as well as the printout of the chart you created.

Answers to Quick Check Questions

SESSION 1.1

1 cell

2 open

3 D2

4 b

5 click the "Sheet2" sheet tab

6 press Ctrl + Home

SESSION 1.2

1 8; D1 + E1 + F1 + G1+ H1 + I1 + J1 + K1

2 B4, B5, B6, C4, C5, C6, D4, D5, D6

3 a. text
   b. value
   c. value
   d. formula
   e. text
   f. formula
   g. text

4 Active sheet(s), Print

5 Print, File

6 c

7 When you exit Excel, the workbook is erased from RAM. So if you want to use the workbook again you need to save it to disk. Click File, then click Save As.

8 press the Delete key

9 revising the contents of one or more cells in a worksheet and observing the effect this change has on all other cells in the worksheet

SESSION 2.1

1 Select the cell where you want the sum to appear. Click the AutoSum button. Excel suggests a formula which includes the SUM function. To accept the formula press the Enter key.

2 =A6+B6

3 cell references. If you were to copy the formula to other cells, these cells are relative references

4 absolute reference

5 Windows clipboard

6 fill-handle

7 double-click the sheet tab, then type the new name, then press the Enter key or click any cell in the worksheet to accept the entry

8 determine the purpose of the worksheet, enter the data and formulas, test the worksheet; correct errors, improve the appearance, document the worksheet, save and print

SESSION 2.2

1 select

2 header

3 Autoformat

4 Click any cell in the row above which you want to insert a row. Click Insert, then click Row

5 c

6 Assuming you are entering a formula with a function, first select the cell where you want to place a formula, type =, the function name and a left parenthesis, then click and drag over the range of cells to be used in the formula. Press the Enter key.

7 click Tools, click Options, then in the View tab, click the Formula check box

8 Landscape

SESSION 3.1

1 a. 13%; b. $0.13

2 Click Format, click Cells; right-click mouse in cell you want to format; use buttons on the Formatting toolbar

3 the data in the cell is formatted with the Comma style using two decimal places

4 Left Align button, Center button, Right Align button, and Merge and Center button

5 Center column headings, right-align numbers, and left-align text

6 Position the mouse pointer over the column header, right-click the mouse and click Column Width. Enter the new column width in the Column Width dialog box. Position the mouse pointer over the right edge of the column you want to modify, then click and drag to increase the column width.

7 Format Painter button

8 The column width of a cell is not wide enough to display the numbers, and you need to increase the column width

SESSION 3.2

1 use the Borders Tab on the Format Cells dialog box, or the Borders button on the Formatting toolbar

2 Click the Drawing button on the Standard toolbar

3 select

4 text box

5 Portrait

6 Click Tools, click View tab, then click the Gridlines check box to remove the check from the check box

7 Excel (graphic) object

SESSION 4.1

1   comparisons among items or changes in data over a period of time

2   selected; also referred to as activated

3   Select the appropriate chart, click Chart Menu, then click Source Data. Click the Collapse dialog box button, then select values to be included in the chart, press the Enter key, then click the OK button

4   Select the chart, move the pointer over the chart area until the pointer changes to an arrow then click and drag to another location on the worksheet

5   select the range of cells to be used as the source of data for the chart

6   the data marker that represents that data point will change to reflect the new value

7   identifies the pattern or colors assigned to the data series in a chart

8   A data point is a value in the worksheet, while the data marker is the symbol (pie slice, column, bar, and so on) that represents the data point in the chart

SESSION 4.2

1   a. a value that originates from a worksheet cell
    b. a slice in a pie chart that represents a single point
    c. a group of related data points plotted in a pie chart that originate from rows or columns in a worksheet

2   Select the A1, then press and hold down the CTRL key and select cells C5 and D10

3   pie chart

4   often, the data you want to plot is not in adjacent cells

5   an embedded chart is a chart object placed in a worksheet and saved with the worksheet when the workbook is saved; a chart sheet is a sheet in a workbook that contains only a chart

6   Select the pie chart you want to rotate, click Chart on the menu bar then click 3-D View to display the 3-D View dialog box. Click either rotate button to rotate the chart.

7   Select the slice you want to "explode," then click and drag the slice away from the center.

8   chart type

Microsoft Excel 97 **Task Reference**

TASK	PAGE #	RECOMMENDED METHOD
AutoComplete, use	E 1.15	To accept Excel's AutoComplete suggestion, press Enter. Otherwise, continue typing a new label.
AutoFormat, use	E 2.29	Select the cells to format, click Format, then click AutoFormat. Select desired format from Table Format list, then click OK.
AutoSum button, use	E 2.9	Click the cell where you want the sum to appear. Click ▣. Make sure the range address in the formula is the same as the range you want to sum.
Border, apply	E 3.20	See Reference Window: Adding a Border.
Cancel action		Press Esc, or click ▣.
Cell contents, clear	E 1.28	Select the cells you want to clear, then press Delete.
Cell contents, copy using Copy command	E 2.15	Select the cell or range you want to copy, then click ▣.
Cell contents, copy using fill handle	E 2.11	Click cell(s) with data or label to copy, then click and drag the fill handle to outline the cell(s) to which the data is to be copied.
Cell reference types, edit	E 2.14	Double-click cell containing formula to be edited. Move insertion point to part of cell reference to be changed, then press F4 until reference is correct, and then press Enter.
Chart title, add or edit	E 4.15 E 4.19	Select the chart. Click Chart, and then click Chart Options. In the Titles tab, click one of the title text boxes, then type the desired title.
Chart, activate	E 4.11	Click anywhere within the chart border. Same as selecting.
Chart, add data labels	E 4.16	Select the chart, then select a single data marker for the series. Click Chart, click Chart Options, then click Data Labels. Select the type of data label you want, then click OK.
Chart, adjust size	E 4.11	Select the chart and drag selection handles.
Chart, apply a pattern to a data marker	E 4.18	See Reference Window: Selecting a Pattern for a Data Marker.
Chart, apply a texture	E 4.28	Click Format Chart Area on Chart toolbar, click Patterns tab, click the Fill Effects button, and then click the Texture tab. Select the desired texture.
Chart, create	E 4.6	Select data to be charted. Click ▣, then complete the steps in the Chart Wizard dialog boxes.
Chart, use picture	E 4.31	Create column or bar chart. Select all columns/bars to be filled with picture, then click Insert, point to Picture, then click From File. Select picture from Insert Picture dialog box, then click OK.
Chart, delete data series	E 4.13	Select the chart, select the data series, then press Delete.
Chart, explode pie slice	E 4.25	Select the pie chart, then click the slice to explode. Drag the selected slice away from center of pie.
Chart, format labels	E 4.27	Select chart labels, then use Formatting toolbar to change font type, size, and style.

Microsoft Excel 97 **Task Reference**

TASK	PAGE #	RECOMMENDED METHOD
Chart, move	E 4.11	Select the chart and drag it to a new location.
Chart, rotate a 3-D chart	E 4.26	Select a 3-D chart. Click Chart, then click 3-D View. Type the values you want in the Rotation and Elevation boxes.
Chart, select	E 4.11	Click anywhere within the chart border. Same as activating.
Chart, update	E 4.12	Enter new values in worksheet. Chart link to data is automatically updated.
Chart Wizard, start	E 4.6	Click 🔳.
Clipboard contents, paste into a range	E 2.15	Click 📋.
Colors, apply to a range of cells	E 3.23	See Reference Window: Applying Patterns and Color.
Column width, change	E 2.24	See Reference Window: Changing Column Width.
Copy formula, use copy-and-paste method	E 2.15	Select the cell with the formula to be copied, click 📋, click the cell you want the formula copied to, then click 📋.
Excel, exit	E 1.32	Click File, then click Exit, or click Excel Close button.
Excel, start	E 1.5	Click the Start button, then point to Programs, if necessary click Microsoft Office, and then click Microsoft Excel.
Font, select	E 3.17	Select the cell or range you want to format. Click Format, click Cells, and then click the Font tab. Select the desired Font from the Font list box.
Font, select size	E 3.17	Select the cell or range you want to format. Click Format, click Cells, and then click the Font tab. Click the Font Size list arrow, then click the desired font size.
Footer, add	E 2.34	In the Print Preview window, click Setup, then click the Header/Footer tab in the Page Setup dialog box. Click the Footer list arrow to choose a preset footer, or click Custom Footer and edit the existing footer in the Footer dialog box.
Format, bold	E 3.16	Select the cell or range you want to format, then click **B**, which toggles on and off.
Format, center text across columns	E 3.15	Select the cell or range with text to center. Click Format, click Cells, then click the Alignment tab. Click the Horizontal Text alignment arrow and select Center Across Selection.
Format, comma	E 3.10	Select the cell or range of cells you want to format, then click 🔳.
Format, copy	E 3.9	Select the cell or range of cells with the format you want to copy. Click 🖌, then select the cell or the range of cells you want to format.
Format, currency	E 3.6	Select the cell or range of cells you want to format. Click Format, then click Cells. Click the Number tab, click Currency in the Category box, then click the desired options.
Format, italic	E 3.17	Select the cell or range you want to format, then click *I* which toggles on and off.

Microsoft Excel 97 **Task Reference**

TASK	PAGE #	RECOMMENDED METHOD
Format, indent text	E 3.15	Select the cell or range you want to indent. Click ▦.
Format, center in cell	E 3.13	Select the cell or range you want to format. Click ▤, which toggles on and off.
Format, font	E 3.16	Select the cell or range you want to format. Click the Font arrow and select the desired font.
Format, percent	E 3.11	Select the cell or range of cells you want to format, then click %.
Format, wrap text	E 3.13	Select the cell or cells you want to format. Click Format, click Cells, then click the Alignment tab. Click Wrap Text check box.
Formula, enter	E 1.17	Click the cell where you want the result to appear. Type = and then type the rest of the formula. For formulas that include cell references, type the cell reference or select each cell using the mouse or arrow keys. When the formula is complete, press Enter.
Formulas, display	E 2.37	Click Tools, then click Options. Click the View tab, then click the Formulas check box.
Function, enter	E 2.21	Type = to begin the function. Type the name of the function in either uppercase or lowercase letters, followed by an opening parenthesis (. Type the range of cells you want to calculate using the function, separating the first and last cells in the range with a colon, as in B9:B15, or drag the pointer to outline the cells you want to calculate. See also Paste Function button, activate.
Gridlines, add or remove	E 3.31	Click Tools, click Options, then click View. Click Gridlines check box.
Header, add	E 2.34	In the Print Preview window, click Setup, then click the Header/Footer tab in the Page Setup dialog box. Click the Header list arrow to select a preset header, or click the Custom Header button to edit the existing header in the Header dialog box.
Help, activate	E 1.26	See Reference Window: Using the Office Assistant, and Figure 1-23.
Labels, enter	E 1.15	Select cell, then type text you want in cell.
Non-adjacent ranges, select	E 4.22	Click the first cell or range of cells to select, then press and hold the Ctrl key as you select the other cell or range of cells to be selected. Release the Ctrl key when all non-adjacent ranges are highlighted.
Numbers, enter	E 1.16	Select the cell, then type the number.
Paste Function button, activate	E 2.19	See Reference Window: Using the Paste Function button.
Patterns, apply to a range of cells	E 3.23	See Reference Window: Applying Patterns and Color.
Print Preview window, open	E 2.30	Click ◘.
Printout, center	E 2.32	In the Print Preview dialog box, click the Setup button. Then click the Margins tab, then click the Horizontally and/or Vertically check boxes.

Microsoft Excel 97 **Task Reference**

TASK	PAGE #	RECOMMENDED METHOD
Printout, landscape orientation	E 3.33	In the Print Preview window, click the Setup button. Then click the Page tab in the Page Setup dialog box, then click the Landscape option button in the Orientation box.
Range, highlight	E 1.18 E 1.28	Position pointer on the first cell of the range. Press and hold the mouse button and drag the mouse through the cells you want, then release the mouse button.
Range, move	E 2.27	Select the cell or range of cells you want to move. Place the mouse pointer over any edge of the selected range until the pointer changes to an arrow �. Click and drag the outline of the range to the new worksheet location.
Range, nonadjacent	E 4.22	See Non-adjacent ranges, select.
Range, select	E 1.18 E 1.28	See Range, highlight.
Row or column, delete	E 2.25	Click the heading(s) of the row(s) or column(s) you want to delete, click Edit, then click Delete.
Row or column, insert	E 2.25	Click any cell in the row/column above which you want to insert the new row/column. Click Insert and then click Rows/Columns. Above the selected range, Excel inserts one row/column for every row/column in the highlighted range.
Sheet tab, rename	E 2.16	Double-click the sheet tab then type the new sheet name.
Sheet, activate	E 1.11	Click the sheet tab for the desired sheet.
Shortcut menu, activate	E 3.24	Select the cells or objects to which you want to apply the command, click the right mouse button, then select the command you want.
Spell check	E 2.23	Click cell A1, then click 🔤.
Text box, add	E 3.27	Click 🄰 on the Drawing toolbar. Position pointer where text box is to appear, then click and drag to outline desired size and shape. Type comment in text box.
Toolbar, add or remove	E 3.25	Click any toolbar with right mouse button. Click the name of the toolbar you want to use/remove from the shortcut menu.
Undo button, activate	E 2.26	Click ↺.
Workbook, open	E 1.11	Click 📂 (or click File, then click Open). Make sure the Look in box displays the name of the folder containing the workbook you want to open. Click the name of the workbook you want to open, then click Open.
Workbook, save with a new name	E 1.21	Click File then click Save As. Change the workbook name as necessary. Specify the folder in which to save workbook in the Save in box. Click Save.
Workbook, save with same name	E 1.21	Click 💾.
Worksheet, close	E 1.31	Click File, then click Close, or click the worksheet Close button.
Worksheet, print	E 1.29	Click 🖨 to print without adjusting any print options. Use the Print command on the File menu to adjust options.